J. M Povey, W. Lancelot Holland

Nunnery Life in the Church of England

Seventeen Years with Father Ignatius

J. M Povey, W. Lancelot Holland

Nunnery Life in the Church of England
Seventeen Years with Father Ignatius

ISBN/EAN: 9783744661164

Printed in Europe, USA, Canada, Australia, Japan

Cover: Foto ©Lupo / pixelio.de

More available books at **www.hansebooks.com**

NUNNERY LIFE

IN THE

CHURCH OF ENGLAND;

OR,

Seventeen Years with Father Ignatius.

BY
SISTER MARY AGNES, O.S.B.

EDITED, WITH PREFACE,
BY THE REV.
W. LANCELOT HOLLAND, M.A.,
Vicar of All Saints', Hatcham.

FOURTH THOUSAND.

London:
HODDER AND STOUGHTON,
27, PATERNOSTER ROW.
———
MDCCCXC.

BUTLER & TANNER,
THE SELWOOD PRINTING WORKS,
FROME, AND LONDON.

CONTENTS.

	PAGE
PREFACE	ix
INTRODUCTION	xxv

CHAPTER I.

MY REASONS FOR BECOMING A SISTER . . . 1

CHAPTER II

CONVENT LIFE ENTERED UPON 17

CHAPTER III.

THE VOW OF POVERTY 28

CHAPTER IV.

THE VOW OF CHASTITY 34

CHAPTER V.

THE VOW OF OBEDIENCE 42

CHAPTER VI.

THE DAWN OF SPIRITUAL LIGHT 49

Contents.

CHAPTER VII.
LIFE AT FELTHAM CONVENT	PAGE 57

CHAPTER VIII.
CONVENT LIFE AT SLAPTON, IN DEVONSHIRE	64

CHAPTER IX.
CONVENT LIFE AT LLANTHONY	79

CHAPTER X.
DAILY ROUTINE AT LLANTHONY	108

CHAPTER XI.
ILL-TREATMENT OF CHILDREN	115

CHAPTER XII.
SOME OF THE LLANTHONY RULES, WITH ACCOMPANYING PENANCES	121

CHAPTER XIII.
OF WHAT RELIGION IS FATHER IGNATIUS?	128

CHAPTER XIV.
MY DEPARTURE FROM LLANTHONY	136

Contents.

CHAPTER XV.

	PAGE
AT LLANTHONY AGAIN	146

CHAPTER XVI.

APPARITIONS AND MIRACLES	158

CHAPTER XVII.

LIBERTY	176

APPENDIX A	193
,, B	197
,, C	199

PREFACE.

IN the summer of last year (1889), I first heard of the authoress of this autobiography: not accidentally, as some might put it, but rather by the good providence of Jehovah, who " worketh all things after the counsel of His own will."

Ex-sister Mary Agnes, or Miss J. M. Povey, had been attending one of Mrs. Edith O'Gorman Auffray's (better known as "The Escaped Nun") lectures at the Town Hall, Kensington, and after the lecture she obtained an interview with the lecturess, during which she gave her a short account of her own experiences in convents nominally connected with the Church of England. The following day I happened to meet Mrs. Auffray, who passed on to me what Miss Povey had told her. I at once made up my mind to request this lady, if possible, to publish her experiences, and I wrote a letter to her offering any assistance in my power, if she entertained the idea of making her experiences more widely known.

I should have mentioned that Mrs. Auffray had recommended Miss Povey to communicate with me, and had urged upon her the importance of bearing witness to the merciful deliverance God had vouchsafed to her.

I feel bound, therefore, to express to Mrs. Auffray my thanks for the good advice she gave Miss Povey; and let me say here that though perhaps no woman has been more vilified, and persecuted, by the Roman Catholics, and I fear too by many Ritualists and weak, half-hearted Protestants, than has Mrs. Auffray, yet no woman has been more blessed by God in exposing the errors of Romanism. To my mind, it is as easy to prove the perfect veracity of Mrs. Auffray's story, told with such power, as it is to prove that once Queen Elizabeth reigned in England, or that the Duke of Wellington led his soldiers to victory when the battle of Waterloo was fought. I had not long to wait before receiving from Miss Povey a small portion of her manuscript; and, being struck with the unaffected style, and genuine appearance of the story thus commenced, I consented at her request to correct and revise, or, in one word, to edit, the whole of the material she might feel disposed to place in my hands.

I need hardly say, considering the many other engagements devolving upon the vicar of a parish of 20,000 people, that I have been obliged to make a somewhat slow progress with the work, short though it may appear, and when I had come to the close of it, I could not but feel that the book was worthy of an editor who could have devoted more time, attention and talent to it, than it was within my reach to do.

I would acknowledge here, with a feeling of deep gratitude, the assistance given me towards the close of my editorial duties, in connection with the book, by a gentleman whose name I am not at liberty to divulge. This gentleman introduced the manuscript to the publishers, and he has most kindly cast his eye carefully over the whole work, correcting or rescinding where he thought it advisable. Perhaps there are few men in England who know more than he does on the subject of English sisterhoods. He has lectured with ability on the subject, and is likely to become ere long a well-known writer. Since I made him acquainted with the work I was editing, and had had some conversation with him upon these matters, I only wished he had taken my place as editor.

I think that those who read through this book will readily acknowledge that Miss Povey has done her work well, and I feel sure she will receive the hearty congratulations of a great number of persons. She has been obliged to write under some considerable disadvantages, arising from the nature of her employment, which does not allow a very wide margin of time for writing; consequently, as she reminded me, she has had no time to look over and correct what force of circumstances compelled her to write somewhat hurriedly.

"I shall be much obliged," she has written to me, "for any improvement you think fit to make, in correcting, revising, rescinding, in all the manuscript." Any excellence that may be found in the book must be wholly due to the authoress; none could have written in the forcible and graphic way she has done, who had not herself passed through so strange and painful an experience.

Preface. xiii

I have only had one interview with Miss Povey, and *that* when the book was well nigh finished. But before then I took great pains to find out the thorough trustworthiness of her antecedents and statements. God forbid that I should ever venture to send before the public a work of such deep import, were I not perfectly convinced that ex-sister Mary Agnes was in a position to write, and actually was writing, the truth, the whole truth, and nothing but the truth.

I have by me a letter written by the Mother Abbess of the Feltham convent, to the lady in whose employment Miss Povey is now living, giving her, as will be acknowledged by all, a very high character for truthfulness and uprightness.

THE CONVENT, FELTHAM,
Sept. 14*th*, 1887.

DEAR MADAM,—

Miss J. M. Povey lived in my house for ten years, and I knew of her before and since.

She bears, and has always borne, the highest moral character; all her relations are highly respectable people. She is thoroughly conscientious and trustworthy, clever and observant, and speaks well. She is a good needlewoman, and I should think quite capable of undertaking what you require of her, and is one who would do her work quite as well in your absence as if you were at home superintending her.

She is *quite above* the ordinary station of domestic servants. There is no mystery in her life.

I am, dear Madam, yours truly,

MARY HILDA.

Miss Povey has also received the two following letters from the same lady :—

THE CONVENT, FELTHAM,
Feb. 15*th*, 1886.

POOR DEAR CHILD,—
I am not in the least surprised at your leaving, and I pity you much for several reasons.

MARY HILDA.

THE CONVENT, FELTHAM,
Feb. 20*th*, 1886.

DEAREST CHILD,—
However good F. Ignatius may be (and he has much goodness), I never thought he had much tact; but that he could be so utterly devoid of it as to tell M. Wereburgh that you knew about her history after leaving here first time, I could not have imagined. Of course, knowing her as I did, I can but feel sure that she was anxious for you to leave, lest you should hint it to others. I am, as I have said, very sorry for you, and hope you will not stay in the world.

Your always sincere friend, and
affectionate Sp. Mother,

MARY HILDA, M. Sup.

Preface. xv

I have ample testimony to the truth of her statement, "*Seventeen* Years with Father Ignatius," since I am able to give the following extract from a letter written by "Ignatius" himself to Sister Mary Agnes, soon after she had left the convent :—

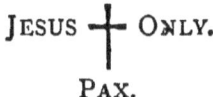

Pax.
LLANTHONY ABBEY,
Dec. 30th, 1884.

MY DEAREST CHILD,—

. . . You have profited nothing from all my teaching and patience of nearly seventeen years: you cannot imagine the grief you have given me.

I have no time for more. I shall always pray for you, and love you, and you must think of me as always

Your affectionate, but disappointed Father,
IGNATIUS, O.S.B.

Most of the readers of this book will probably know the meaning of the letters "O.S.B." They mean the "Order of St. Benedict." Now, although Sister Mary Agnes never became what is called in conventual phraseology a "*professed*" nun in that Order, that is to say, she never "took the black veil," yet for all these years she was a *novice nun*, and was always looked upon and called a *nun*.

In a letter Father Ignatius wrote to her in the year 1879, whilst she was in the convent, this sentence occurs: " You are really a little *nun*"; and again: "If I find you really grown in a nun-like spirit, I really hope we may fix (D.V.) your profession, say, this year."

I might very easily add more to prove that this simple story of seventeen years of convent life is not a fabricated one, but the evidence I have produced, out of a mass which I have at my disposal, will surely be enough.

Miss Povey has decided to make known her life as a nun, in order that others may take warning, and profit by her experiences. No young lady who may become acquainted with this book can ever say, should she be deluded into taking the veil, that she took that terrible leap, as I fear many do take it, in the dark.

Convents, or sisterhoods, in connection with the Church of England, are by no means few and far between, and it is to be hoped that this book will bring conviction to many of the transparent fact, that the teaching and practices within their walls are not so widely different from the same within the walls of Roman Catholic convents.

I hope that Miss Povey's work may do good in making known the danger of being misled by the *apparently* pure evangelical teaching which Father Ignatius is said to give. Now, it seems to me, that here in this book we have the means of subjecting this specious-looking metal to a severe test. His so-called Gospel sermons and orations contain some good metal with which the counterfeit coin is covered and made to pass as genuine.

It is an incumbent duty to let her revelations be known far and wide, so that souls be not led astray.

Is there not a cause? Consider it, I beg of you, who may read this book. Remember that with scarcely an exception (I don't think the infallibility of the Pope is acknowledged in these convents) every Roman Catholic tenet is unblushingly held and taught in the three convents which tnis book refers to. Roman Catholic literature of the most advanced type is constantly used in them.

Another advantage that I hope and feel sure

b

will arise from studying this little book, will be found in the remarkably clear definition Miss Povey has been enabled to give of the three celebrated and essentially Romish *vows* of poverty, chastity, and obedience. These self-same vows are just now being spoken of a good deal, and many are telling us that they are to be an essential element in the new brotherhoods which the Bishop of Rochester has so lately, in the Upper House of Convocation and in his Triennial Charge, advocated. I cannot but hope that God has raised up, at a most opportune moment, a witness against the imposition of such vows, whether on men or women. I hope it may lead those who are favourable to the scheme to favour it no more. Is it not palpable to all that just as sisterhoods are made the secret repositories of extreme Romish education, practices, and literature, so likewise will brotherhoods be made to serve a similar purpose?

We are certainly living in "perilous times," and it is amazing to behold the spirit of indifference in quarters where we might least expect it, not only with regard to the great strides Ritualism is making, so that Protestant Evangelicalism is well nigh eclipsed, but this indifference is as great with regard to the advance of Romanism and Jesuitism,[1] and (saddest result of all) to the building of so many hundreds of Roman Catholic convents and monasteries in the United Kingdom.

There are in existence societies for the prevention of cruelty to children, and for the prevention of cruelty to animals; but although the cruelties and tortures, called penances, which are inflicted on many a poor helpless nun are greater than those inflicted on animals, the man who raises up his voice against this worst form of inhumanity is counted unloving and bigoted. Believe me, the unloving ones are those who lend any countenance whatever to, or who do not make a righteous protest against, the conventual and monastic *system*, according to which disciplines, hair-shirts, scourgings, and various other forms of cruelty and degradation are employed.

---

[1] I read as follows in the October number of the *Protestant Observer*:—"I remember hearing Father Ignatius tell an Oxford audience some years ago that he was called Ignatius, not after the famous Father of the early Church, but 'after my patron-saint, Ignatius Loyola, founder of the Jesuit Order.' May we not call him Ignatius Loyola the Second?"

Preface.

Do we not see that, if this system is allowed to advance in the Church of England, these very penances (many of which *do* exist, all of which *may* exist, in the Church of England convents), which, without any doubt, exist in Romish convents, will be inflicted with equal severity in English Church convents.

Sister Mary Agnes does not speak of prison-like underground cells in Father Ignatius's convents, and we believe, therefore, that anyhow at present they do not exist in them. But she does speak of penances, and she has felt them.

In bringing my Preface to a close, I will give a statement with regard to the Church of England convent in Woodstock Road, in the City of Oxford, founded by the late Dr. Pusey. This statement has been made by a clergyman of the Established Church, who is perfectly prepared, if need be, to give his name.

In the summer of 1866, I was travelling from Oxford to London, and there happened to be in the same railway carriage one of the leading tradesmen in the city of Oxford.

Our conversation turned upon the advances which Romanism was apparently making in the United Kingdom,

Preface. xxi

and conspicuously by the influence of a certain section now well known as Ritualists in our own Church.

He asked me if I had noticed a building which was being erected in "The Parks" (Oxford), and whether I was aware that owing to a clause in the lease of the ground, and some complications arising therefrom, the owners of the edifice had determined even, if necessary, to surrender the lease, and transfer the materials to a freehold site in another part of the city? I remarked that such a course looked suspicious, made my own comments on it, and, when opportunity offered, acted.

During a stay in Oxford a few days subsequently, I went one afternoon to see for myself, and on coming to the building, asked the clerk of the works, or foreman, if I might look round it. Having done so, I found the fabric almost completed, but was struck by an apparent loss of space owing to the height of the walls from the ground, without any ostensible object. I observed a small door, directly underneath the main entrance, and on examination found it padlocked, but seeing that the staple was not clenched, I removed it with the point of my umbrella, and thus gained entrance to what proved to be a long corridor, right and left of which *cells* were erected, but not completed.

As rapidly as I could I took a general survey of the whole arrangements, replaced the staple and padlock, and before leaving expressed my best thanks to the foreman, who was engaged with some workmen in a shed at the entrance to the premises, erected quite apart from the building.

I then talked with him about the peculiar construction of the building, and asked him why the walls were built so as to leave a great space between the foundations and first floor. He stated that this was for *the purpose of ventilation* only. I then remarked that it was unusual to see buildings so constructed, and then I said, "Was that all?" He volunteered the statement that there was nothing in this space underneath the fabric but the external walls. Happening to know differently, I drew my own conclusions, and left.—(Signed) ——.

Finally, let us hope that God's people throughout England will make it a matter of daily intercession to the throne of Grace that convents, whether Anglican or Roman Catholic, may be utterly abolished. I sincerely trust that this book will be read as a witness of what God's good providence and sovereign grace have done for the writer of this interesting narrative, and therefore can do for others. May the Spirit of the living God that opened the eyes of Sister Mary Agnes, be poured out abundantly to open the eyes of many in this land, who are sitting in darkness and the shadow of death. And may they be led, by the same Spirit, through the one only Mediator between God and man, even Jesus Christ, to obtain fellowship with the Father, together with all other spiritual blessings in Christ Jesus, "according as God hath chosen us in Him before the foundation of the world." And, finally, may He also enable them to "stand fast in the liberty wherewith Christ hath made them free."

W. LANCELOT HOLLAND.

All Saints' Vicarage,
   Hatcham Park, S.E.,
      February, 1890.

INTRODUCTION.

IN sending forth this book to the world, I would have it clearly understood that it is not my desire to injure any one. I only wish that *the mistakes of my life* may prove a warning to others and prevent them from taking the step I did. I feel it to be a solemn duty, which I owe to God, to put before the public convent life in the Church of England, as I found it.

Naturally I shrink from the task, for the Mother of the Feltham convent has always acted, as far as my experience goes, conscientiously, and it was in no way on her account that I felt bound to withdraw from convent life. Besides Father Ignatius himself *once* seemed to love me as his "little daughter," and was exceedingly kind to me. Let it be remembered that I was *then* but a child and a very simple and inexperienced one.

In one sense, it is not against him personally

that I am writing, yet, in another, it is, because he was head over all, added to which, he made a personal application to my mother to give me up to him for God's service, and thus he was responsible for seeing that my life was made at least endurable; instead of which, he gave me up entirely into the hands of a certain Mother Superior, who (I would speak the truth in love) was a zealous and tyrannical woman.

Believing it, then, to be my duty, I now take up my pen, and may God guide it, so that, in His hands, it may be the means of saving young girls and women, and young men and boys, from inflicting on their relatives the bitter pain and sorrow which I caused my own dear mother and friends. May many by this warning be saved from the bitter disappointment which was my lot, when I found convent life *so* different in practice and reality from what in theory and fancy it seemed to be. Instead of it being the "Gate of Heaven," as it is sometimes said to be, my experience was that it is much nearer another gate.

I feel convinced too that, if the truth could only

Introduction. xxvii

be got at, it would be discovered that my experience was not an exceptional one. I have heard that it was St. Chrysostom who said, "A monk, by the very nature of the life he leads, is either an angel or a devil," and I seldom, if ever, knew a monk or boy, a girl or woman, who, sooner or later, did not turn into something which was far removed from that which is angelic, though at their entrance into that name of "Pax," they were, to all appearances, "perfect saints."

Instead of being ennobled by the monastic and conventual life, my experience has been (and I have had an experience of some seventeen years, and have come in contact with a goodly number of persons living under vows) that the life is far from having an ennobling influence. Life of this kind generally causes those who lead it to become mean, petty, and selfish, and no selfishness can equal a nun's, particularly when nature inclines her to be so.[1] Nuns are either crushed slaves *or*

---

[1] "There are persons, even amongst 'Religious,' so insensible to the sorrows and sufferings of others, that we might ask whether they possess a human heart" ("Thoughts and Suggestions for [Ritualistic] Sisters of Charity," page 81. London: Hodges, 1871)..

tyrants, and often so puffed up with pride that they look upon "seculars" as a race of beings far below themselves, and who, as the Lady Prioress Wereburgh used to say to us, "should think themselves highly honoured to have the privilege of a nun condescending to speak to them."

I would ask all who read this story to overlook the lack of style and order which may be apparent, but I am now very much occupied in earning my bread, and can only give a few night-hours occasionally to the task, and I have never been accustomed to work of this kind.

CHAPTER I.

MY REASONS FOR BECOMING A SISTER.

FROM the earliest time that my memory goes back, I loved Jesus, though I knew very little about Him—only what my dear mother taught me, and she was what is termed a "shy Christian." But I often wished that people would talk more about Him, at least to me; and as a little girl I used to look at people, and wish they would speak to me of Jesus, though I was too timid to put my thoughts into words.

When I was about fourteen years of age, in the year 1868, there was a great stir about a new preacher who preached at several city churches, including St. Edmund's, Lombard Street, and St. Ethelburga's, Bishopsgate. His name was Father Ignatius; he was a Church of England clergyman, and called himself a monk. At that period I happened to be on a visit to my aunt, and my sister wrote and told me that Father Ignatius preached monasticism, that he had a monastery and would soon open a convent. I remember how I thought everybody was turning to Roman Catholicism; and I made up my mind not to go near this strange man. So at first I would not go to hear him, though somehow I was very anxious to see him. At last my mother persuaded me to go, and I heard him preach the love of Jesus as I had never before heard it. I recollect how my mother presented me to him, and how he took my hand, and said, "God bless you, dear child!" Though he said neither more nor less I was won, and from that moment I felt compelled to dwell on all his doings, and to drink in his words. What extraordinary power, or *mesmerism*, is it that this man possesses, enabling him to exert such an influence, not only over a simple child, but also over young and old, man and woman, noble and peasant? How often have I asked myself this question, yet in the course of twenty years I have not solved the mystery! But does he retain the friendship of those he wins? For a short time he does, but as a rule they eventually turn away from him, and sometimes even become his greatest enemies; for he possesses a strange power not only of winning love, but also of casting it away from him when won.

But I have somewhat departed from my story, which I will now resume. I remember being in church one evening, and we sang the words:

> The love of Jesus, what it is
> None but His loved ones know.

I thought to myself, "Who are His loved ones?" Day after day I went about wondering who they were. I would look into every face I met, but the love of Jesus did not seem to me stamped there; yet I was determined to find out, for, I said to myself, "I *must* be His loved one!" At last I saw a gentle, pale-faced sister; and she looked so good and pure (my favourite text was, "Blessed are the pure in heart") that a sudden thought flashed into my mind that it was these sisters, or nuns, who were the "loved ones," and that therefore I must be a sister. But I was not bold enough to tell any one my thoughts, besides which I thought I was very much too young to be a nun. I recollect that just at this time I went to some private meetings,[1] held by certain sisters, and one of them asked me, on one of these occasions, "Should you like to be a sister?" My heart jumped on hearing the question, and I replied, "Yes." No more was said then; but when I again went, Father Ignatius asked me the same question, and I made the same reply as before. He then told me to ask my mother to allow me to be "*given to God*" as a nun. Of course my mother would not hear of it, and only laughed at me, and called me "a goose to want to shut myself away from mother and everybody." The idea, however, had so taken possession of me, that I begged over and over again to be allowed to go; but my mother would not give her consent. Every time Father Ignatius saw me he asked if I had obtained my mother's consent, and I was obliged to say "No." One day, I remember, he said to me,

---

[1] These were held in Hunter Street, Brunswick Square; the sisters were of the third order, or associate sisters, living in the world, but wearing a dress similar to that in my photograph. They used to accompany Father Ignatius when he went to preach or attend meetings of a more private character in Hunter Street. It was at one of these meetings that I first met the Feltham Mother, early in the year 1868.

"Well, ask your mother to let you *go for a month on a visit!*" I dared not ask her for a month, knowing she would not grant me so long a time, so I asked her to let me go for a week, and after considering my request for two days, she told me I might go for a week. I therefore went for that period. I was fifteen years of age then; and the convent was at Feltham, where I stayed for ten years. But before the week had expired, I asked for another week, saying I was so happy in this new life. To my request she made answer, "Another week, but not a day over." During this week the Father called upon my mother, and persuaded her to "give me to God." Very reluctantly she gave her consent, as she told me, "for one year, to sicken you of it, and you will soon be glad to come back home to your mother." No one but God ever knew for years after how I longed to get back to my mother, though I dared not allow it even to myself. When my mother gave me up, she had Father Ignatius's promise not to let me take life-vows until I was twenty-one or twenty-five years of age.

The first year passed away very happily. I was

young; and being small in stature, I was made a pet of, until another young sister came. Then the Mother changed, and she who had so petted me suddenly took a dislike to me; not that she was so very unkind. But how I yearned to be loved! No one seemed to love me, and I loved her, oh, so much! When I went up to her and said, "Mother, dear," instead of opening her arms, and folding me in them as she used to do, she would turn away with a shudder. Why she did this, I never knew. I could not fail to feel surprise at it, as she had often taught me that "a spiritual father's, and mother's, and sister's love is far greater than that of any earthly parents." I was sure my mother would never thus turn away from me. Oh, how keenly I felt this coldness! and when I went to bed, I would cry and sob for hours, knowing that no one in that house loved me, and my heart seemed fit to break at such a loveless life. My mother's smile, her words, and her every look and action, would rise up before me. I remembered my sister and dear little brother, both of whom I so fondly loved, and I would think, "Oh! if it was not wicked of me, I wish I was home"; but I would then blame myself for thinking thus, for I considered it showed unfaithfulness to God to allow such thoughts even for a moment, and I was afraid lest God should take my "holy vocation" from me, and I would also remember how God would have His spouse forsake all other love that she may love Him, and be His alone.

Was there ever a more cruel and bitter mistake? Cruel is the teaching which requires a young girl to separate herself from the dear good mother, whom God has given her, in order that she may, as is falsely said, serve God without hindrance. What folly and delusion is it that takes possession of us, to think that we can get nearer to God, be more pure, more holy in this life, and be brought to greater glory in the next life, by shutting oneself up in a particular house and never going out except to the garden, I cannot fathom!

Listen to the text which brings us up to this unnatural life, or, as we were told, this "supernatural life." "A garden inclosed is My sister, My spouse; a spring shut up," etc. Year after year this text bears us up, coupled with the thought that such a life is only a short time in comparison with eternity, when we shall reap the great reward of our life of self-sacrifice. Blinder than the very heathen was I!

Sometimes I would stand and look around that small enclosure and think, "Shall I never in this life go farther than this garden surrounded with trees?" Often my brain seemed to turn at the very thought. If only I could have seen a great space, or a great sea, it would be better; but there were those trees in a flat country, and nothing beyond (a true type indeed). But then I would come back to my text, as above quoted, and think that as God is pleased with me, nothing else is of consequence. So I went on year after year, anything but happy, yet not *daring* to let myself think of turning back. Often did I LONG to speak of mother and of the dear ones at home, but I could not without breaking the rule, "never to speak of our earthly relations except to God in prayer." If we broke this rule, we had to confess it the same day, and perform the prescribed penance of losing the hour's recreation, do some menial work, and keep silence during the only hour we had set apart for conversation.

At the end of my first year my mother wrote to Father Ignatius demanding me back. She wrote to me at the same time, telling me she was coming to fetch me; but the Father gave me no advice on the subject, and I could have gone back as far as consent from my superiors went. At that time they gave me my mother's letter, which of course they had read (all letters are read by the Mother first); but what about the teaching and instruction that had gone before? What about the awful words I had heard that, "should I ever even look back, I should then be unmeet for the kingdom of God"? What about the example of Lot's wife, so often set before us? She only *looked* back, and how terrible the *immediate* result! What would happen (I thought) to one espoused to Christ, if she not only looked back, but deliberately turned from the "path that leads to life," as we were instructed? Not even for one second did I *dare* to allow myself to think it. I would not go back, and did not.

My mother waited another year, and came this time to the convent without writing, so that I might not be influenced beforehand. Oh!

mothers, little do you know the influence that is always at work: and yet your children dare not even wish to tell you, for it would be a terrible sin to tell even you anything about that influence, —it would be a grave scandal to do so. But it is equally a great sin to hide anything from our *Superior;* we are distinctly told never to conceal anything, not even our most secret thoughts, from our Superior. Should we have a great temptation to leave the life we had entered on, or any great temptation to rebel against convent rules, we were expressly told to make it known at once, that we might have the benefit of our Superior's advice. Remember, too, that self-examination comes three times a day!

One morning, at the Communion, the Father suddenly turned round, saying:

"If any sister in this chapel has one single unfaithful thought of going back to the world, *I dare* her to come to this altar, and touch with her lips the sacred Body and Blood of her God. 'Woe be to him through whom the offence cometh!'"

We were all startled, and I said, "Lord, is it I?" But it was not me, for I would rather have suffered torture than commit so great a sin. A certain lay-sister stayed behind at that time, and I asked her, when the next opportunity offered itself to me, if she had thoughts of looking back? She replied:

"I told the reverend Father last night, I thought I ought to go home to my father to keep house for him, as my mother was dead."

The reader will perceive that though we were not shut in by literal bolts and bars, we were bound by something very, very much more effectual—even by the nameless and unexplainable fear of being guilty of the *terrible sin* of going back to the world. How fearfully real and effectual is this feeling!

My mother and sister then came to fetch me, and I was sent alone into the parlour, that they might see how little I was *apparently* influenced by any outside pressure, and that I might tell them that I had a wish of my own free will to remain in the convent. At this interview, some one, unknown to my mother, was, of course, within earshot, according to rule; but I did not fear that, for I had no intention of going back, and thus losing the virgin's crown in heaven, which I so much coveted, and which could only be obtained, as I then supposed, by remaining true to my holy calling. My sister was evidently exercising great self-restraint at this interview, and could scarcely refrain from weeping; my own mother sobbed, and my heart was wrung, and yet I dared not think of going home. Almost choking with emotion, and stretching out my arms and folding them around my mother's neck, I gasped :

"Mother, darling, I DO love you ; but I belong to God, and I *dare* not go back."

Tears blind me, even now while I write, as I think of that *awful* struggle, which I had been taught was right and pleasing to God. At last my mother was able to speak, and she said :

"This is the second time I have tried to get you away, and you refuse to come. Now, mind, I shall never come to see you again, or write to you, but you will live to repent the day you ever shut yourself up in a convent, and remember that I will have nothing more to do with you while you are here; but if ever you should want a home, while I have one, it is yours also."

She went on to say:

"Father Ignatius will get tired of you some day, then what will you do if your mother is no more?"

My reply was (remembering what a great pet he made of me, and also how I had read and been told that "the love of spiritual parents was so much stronger than that of any earthly parent"):

"You are, dear mother, very kind; but I am sure the reverend Father will never change."

And so I truly thought.

This wrench from all home-ties well nigh broke my heart; yet I dared not even think of leaving the convent, though in my heart of hearts I deeply wished I had never taken up that "golden plough." Ah! had I only not taken it up, there would have been no sin in wishing for home again; but now it was far different, for it seemed to me, at the time, that in God's great goodness the path had been shown to me down which I must walk, and that I must with determination choose the good, and cast aside every thought of returning to the world. And so I chose what I had been taught was the good, and no one until now knows the bitter struggle I passed through. How often did I recall this day, or rather I could not drive it from my memory whilst sleeping or waking! It often drove sleep from my eyes, and my constant thought was, "If only I could put my arms round my mother's neck, and kiss her just once more!"

At last all was arranged for me to take the black veil, and I even had orders to write for my mother to come and see this imposing ceremony, as it is really a novice's entire *death* to the world, and we are allowed to see our nearest relative before we die. I was told I might go into the visitor's room to see my mother if she came; but though my Superior said it was *lawful* to see her, yet she *advised me not to go*, as it might prove a cause of great distraction. When I was first told I might go into the room where my mother was to come, my heart leaped for joy. "Now," I thought, "I shall be able to kiss her once again." But then I remembered all the advice I had been given, and I wanted to be "perfect"; so, for the love of Jesus, as *I thought*, I gave up the privilege and joy of kissing my own dear mother!

As a rule, we only saw friends behind the grille,

with a third person, who must be a professed nun, to listen and report us should we make a slip in our conversation, or scandalize a secular by repeating anything that should not be told.

However, after all, my taking the black veil and thus becoming a professed nun was put off, as the superiors could not agree as to what place I was to take in the community. The reverend Mother wished me to keep where I was—the reverend Father wished me to be raised above six or seven who were older, and had been professed some years back. Since neither would waive their wishes, I had to wait, and consequently, I never took the black veil, or *life*-vows, and *never* saw my mother again, as when I left convent life she was not alive.

CHAPTER II.

CONVENT LIFE ENTERED UPON.

IN the beginning of November, 1868, I went on a short visit to the "Benedictine convent of cloistered nuns," at Feltham. Father Ignatius, who claims to be the father, founder, and reviver of monasticism in the Church of England, had turned an old farm-house at Feltham into a convent.

The "rule" given to the nuns by him can be procured at any Roman Catholic publishers. It is entitled "The Holy Rule of St. Benedict, translated by a Priest of Mount Melleray." There are other translations of the rule, but this one is much more strict than any other which I have read.

After a time Father Ignatius gave us forty-nine observances to keep. These were really much stricter than the rule itself, and they were to be read every day, and the least transgression had to be written down and sent in to our Superior at the close of each week, in addition to the usual confession to a priest. The Feltham Mother never wished us to make a confession to her, though the Mother at Llanthony insisted upon everything being disclosed to her.

To these forty-nine observances, later on, were added about forty-nine more, so that we were hedged all round by them, sleeping or waking. Transgressions of these observances were "convent sins." I have already related how my visit for a week was soon lengthened out, and I will not particularize those first and early experiences.

It was in February, 1869, that I was received into Feltham convent as a postulant. There is a form to go through when a postulant is received. The Superior asks:

> What dost thou desire of us?
> *Postulant.*—To be admitted into the house of God.
> *Superior.*—None can enter our gates but such as seek to be the spouse of the Lamb.
> *Postulant.* — I postulate for the habit of the heavenly espousals in the Holy Order of St. Benedict.
> *Superior.*—Dost thou promise to obey the rules?
> *Postulant.*—I do.

Convent Life Entered Upon. 19

After a few more questions and answers, I was properly made a postulant, and thought myself at heaven's gate.

On April 13th, two months after my reception as a postulant, I took, as a novice, the three conventual vows of poverty, chastity, and obedience. I would remind those of my readers who may be ignorant of these things, that whilst the vow of obedience is put last in order, yet it is of the first importance. I remember well the day I took these vows. I was attired in white, and wore a bridal veil and wreath. I recollect that another girl (Florence S—— by name) stood with me—I should rather say knelt. Together we waited to sacrifice ourselves upon the altar of God, —not by the sacrificial knife, that would be but the work of a few seconds—but by the daily and hourly sacrifice of everything that we loved.

When some of the difficulties and trials of my new life were set before me, I had no fears. I was in a state of high joy at the thought which had been burnt into my soul, viz., that I was espoused to the King of kings, and that I was the Lamb's bride now and for ever. How could fear ruffle my spirit whilst under this spell? Besides, how should a girl of my age (I was but fifteen at this time) have any notion of what sorrow, and trial, and trouble meant, especially, as was the case with me, when an affectionate mother had lovingly and carefully concealed from me any evils that might come in after years?

The anticipation of any evil in the future seemed, however, to fade into insignificance, since I was uplifted above terrestrial things by—I really know not how best to describe it—by the thought of Him whom I regarded as my heavenly Lover. Never did any girl or woman love her lover or her husband more than I did the Lord Jesus Christ, whose bride I *thought* myself to be, *because* I had taken those three vows of poverty, chastity, and obedience. I sometimes felt as if I must die; so overpowered was I with love that I could scarcely breathe.

Often since that time have I asked myself, "What was it that I so loved?" If it had been the love of the heavenly Bridegroom, that seemed as it were to saturate me, would that sister who knelt at my side on this occasion have been permitted in after years to make my life such a misery to me, that I could no longer live a cloistered life? What or who it was I know not; all I know is that whoever or whatever it was, it obtained possession of my first love—the undivided love of my whole being; but that love is gone, and I do not think I could ever love with the same full, pure, and intense love again. That love, fixed on a lover existing only in the imagination, and impressed on my plastic and youthful mind, carried me through a convent experience lasting for seventeen years. And then it vanished. The illusion was dissipated, the *ignis fatuus* was quenched, and I was left alone in my misery, and it seemed, for a time, that nowhere could I find the loved one for whom everything and every one had been sacrificed; but better for me was this misery than that fool's paradise.

But I must return to my story, after this digression, which, however, I hope many youthful readers may peruse and take warning from. My companion and I knelt, as I have mentioned; and thus, upon our knees, we waited for the august ceremony attending ever this mock marriage. All heaven seemed to open, and all of earth seemed to be passing away. I recollect that, after many questions had been put to, and responses made by us, and when sweet words, set to sweeter music, had been sung, there reached our ears some such words as these:

The Bridegroom would have His bride leave father, mother, houses, lands, and all earthly loves, in order that, as the apostle saith, she may be one spirit with Him. My daughter, canst thou do this?

To this we made reply severally:

In His strength I leave all, that I may follow Christ.

Then the reverend Father uttered these words:

Beware, my daughter, before putting thy hand to the golden plough, for *cursed* shalt thou be if perchance thou lookest back.

To which the novice then replied:

I should then be unfit for the kingdom of God,

and repeated the words of Scripture:

When any one voweth a vow unto the Lord, he shall do all that proceedeth out of his mouth (Num. xxx. 2) ;[1]

and again we quoted Ecclesiastes v. 4.

---

[1] If the reader will look at the last verse of this chapter in the Book of Numbers, he will see that the vows there spoken of can have no connection with convent vows, nor can they supply any authority for them. We read in the last verse: "These are the statutes which the Lord commanded Moses between a man and his wife, between the father and his

Convent Life Entered Upon.

After which there was sung in sweetest music, three times over:

To obey is better than sacrifice, and to hearken than the fat of rams: promise unto the Lord your God, and keep it.

I truly imagined that I was vowing to the Lord; and I had heard that God was love, and that therefore it must be sweet to obey His voice, and so I willingly vowed unto the Lord in these words:

1. I vow *holy poverty*, that I will possess nothing as my own, or receive aught, save at the hands of my Superiors, or with their permission. So help me, God. Amen.

2. I vow *holy chastity* during the time of my noviciate. So help me, God. Amen.

3. I vow entire, unquestioning, and absolute obedience to the Father and Mother Superior, during the term of my noviciate. So help me, God. Amen.

My bridal veil was then removed, and my hair cut off quite short; then I retired, and put on the serge habit of a nun, and came back, and I had placed upon me the scapular of obedience, the cord of chastity, and the sandals of poverty. Be-

daughter, being yet in her youth in her father's house." Please note this. Oh, how clever and subtle are some people in twisting Scripture and wresting it from its proper bearing!—EDITOR.

sides these, I again put on the nun's veil and bridal wreath. My companion and myself were then given new names. I, Jane Mary Povey, was called "Sister Mary Agnes of the Holy Child Jesus"; Florence S—— was called "Sister Mary Wereburgh of the Blessed Sacrament."

The following hymn was then sung, which I must give in full, as it affords such an insight into the *delusion* of convent life. I believe Father Ignatius is the writer of this hymn :

Farewell, thou world of sorrow,
Unrest, unpeace, and strife ;
I leave thee for the threshold
Of the celestial life.

Farewell, world of sadness;
Farewell, earthly joys ;
Lo ! my heart is seeking
Bliss that never cloys.

Strains of heavenly music,
Sights surpassing fair,
Steal upon my senses,
Fall upon mine ear.

Joy of ageless gladness,
Peace that none can tell,
Banishes all sadness,
Satisfies me well.

Languishing for Jesus,
   Longing for His love ;
Thus I'll journey onwards,
   To my home above.

Body, soul, and spirit,
   To my Lord I give ;
Yearning to behold Him,
   Dying whilst I live.

In the lone, still night-watch,
   'Mid the noon-tide light,
Yearns my soul for Jesus ;
   Here it seems all night.

Pant I for the morning,
   And the day-star's gleam,
When in endless sunshine
   Dies earth's weary dream.

Upwards, then, and onwards,
   Soars my joyful soul
Jesus' arms are open,
   Jesus' heart my goal.

Then my Love shall kiss me,
   Call me all His own,
Wrap me in His brightness,
   Rest me near His throne.

Smiling fondly on me,
   Mindful of this day,
When I vowed me to Him,
   I shall joy for aye !

'Mid the throng of virgins,
  In the lily's vale,
Where our Spouse is feeding,
  Sunbeams never pale.

All is love and beauty—
  Jesus, He is there;
All is peace and pleasure,
  All surpassing fair.

Alleluia! chant we,
  In our convent praise;
Shadowing forth the hymnals,
  Which we then shall raise.

Praise we now the Father,
  With the glorious Son;
Praise to God the Spirit
  Likewise shall be done.   Amen.

During the singing of this hymn the newly made novice kneels, and all the sisters come, with lighted tapers, to kiss and embrace their new sister; after which a procession is formed, tapers are carried, incense is burnt, and these words are sung:

The wise virgins took oil in their lamps; they went in with Him to the marriage, and the door was shut.

These words were scarcely finished, when a door was suddenly and loudly slammed; and it seemed hard to realize that we were still in the flesh, and there came to my heated imagination some strange expectation of the beatific vision.

No wonder that brains are turned, and young and inexperienced hearts are deluded and led astray by such an imposing ceremony, which no words of mine can adequately describe. You must have been on the spot fully to realize it.

I would impress very strongly on all who read these pages a fact that I think is not generally known, viz., that there is in the convent no difference whatever between a novice and a black-veiled or fully professed nun with regard to vows or rule, save that the latter vows for life, and the novice for a time. Yet the novice believes that she has no more right in the sight of God to go back from her vows than a life-vowed nun has.

CHAPTER III.

THE VOW OF POVERTY.

I PURPOSE now to write a short chapter on the Vow of Poverty. By this vow a nun has stripped herself of everything; she no longer possesses the right to use anything, or any member of her body, without the permission of her superior. Body and soul, hands, eyes, and feet, are all given up; therefore the nun may not use her hands or her feet even to perform a kind and helpful action for her fellow-nuns, without first going to ask the leave of her Superior. Often, especially at first, I did not understand my obligation, and consequently I would act without permission, and bring upon myself the necessity of performing some penance, that my sin might thus be atoned for. A nun may be almost parched with thirst, yet she must not drink even a cup of cold water without first finding the Superior and asking her leave, and

The Vow of Poverty.

even then she may not obtain it ; and if leave is granted, she may be censured for her alleged want of mortification. The nun who has taken this vow of poverty must never possess or make use of anything which has not been either given or lent to her by the Superior, neither can she borrow or lend anything without leave. This kind of existence really engendered the most abominable selfishness, and I never saw any selfishness to equal a nun's. Her vow of poverty makes her selfish. She has nothing but what is doled out scantily by her Superior; and when she does get anything, she takes good care to keep it, not knowing when she will receive the like again. This does not apply to anything great and valuable, but such trifles as pins and needles, or cotton, or a piece of paper, or a flower-pot. To give or lend a flower, a picture, a thimble, a needle, a book, or anything else, without leave, is to break the Vow of Poverty, for which confession must be made, and reparation by public penance.

Anything sent by the parents or relations of the nuns may be disposed of as the Superior likes; and should it be given to another nun, we were told, "Let the sister for whom that gift was sent beware of murmuring at her Superior's wisdom." Often did I have presents taken from me, without form or ceremony, and given to another, my face being carefully watched whilst the transfer was being made, to see how I bore the trial, or if I betrayed any signs of criticising the actions of my Superior.[1]

I remember that once a dear little child was brought into our community; and being very fond

---

[1] In "The Rule of our Most Holy Father St. Benedict," edited, with English translation and explanatory notes, by a monk of St. Benedict's Abbey, Fort Augustus, occur these words, which show that the rules which regulate the convents connected with this Order are very similar to those regulating the monasteries of the same order in the Church of Rome:

"By no means let a monk be allowed to receive, either from his parents, or any one else, or from his brethren, letters, tokens, or any gifts whatsoever, or to give them to others, without permission of the abbot. And if anything be sent to him, even by his parents, let him not presume to receive it, until it hath been made known to the abbot. *But even if the abbot order it to be received, it shall be in his power to bid it to be given to whom he pleaseth, and let not the brother to whom it may have been sent be grieved, lest occasion be given to the devil. Should any one, however, presume to act otherwise, let him be subjected to the discipline of the Rule*" (p. 155).—EDITOR.

The Vow of Poverty. 31

of children, and thinking of my brothers, I held out my arms to the child, and was on the point of kissing him, when I heard the authoritative voice of the rev. Father, saying, "Sister Agnes, sit down. Not without leave; you should ask first." I coloured as if accused of some great crime, and sat down, but was too ashamed when recreation time came to ask to kiss him then. I had only been a novice for a few months, and did not think of my vow of poverty being broken by using my arms, or lips, or will, without leave.

Another time—it was at Christmas—I saved a mince-pie to give away to the first poor person who came to the door. I was portress then. An old man came, and I related at recreation how pleased he was with my gift; but, alas! I brought down upon myself a little lecture, and was told that I had no right to give convent property away. "But," said I, "it was mine—my very own." Whereupon I learnt that for me the words "mine" and "thine" did not exist, since by this vow of poverty everything belonged to the Father Superior.

We might not even borrow a pocket-handkerchief, though, as we were allowed but three, it was often very necessary to borrow one, for we could not without permission even wash them without breaking rule. If a sister brought with her several dozens, they would be distributed according to the needs of the community, and the rest put away for future use, as the new novice would be breaking her vow by retaining more than she needed for present use.

We were very fortunate in being allowed pocket-handkerchiefs at all. I know another English sisterhood where the nuns are only allowed hard blue-checked dusters, and as the rev. Father and Mother and sisters have the disgusting habit of snuff-taking, they must find these dusters very inconvenient.

Should we use any other article in lieu of a pocket-handkerchief, it must be confessed, and reparation made by holding such article up high at the Magnificat, in the presence of the Blessed Sacrament, so that all who were assembled might see that we had robbed God of what we had promised.

Again, if we broke any article, or put it to an

The Vow of Poverty. 33

improper use, the penance consisted in placing the said article, or piece of it, upon the head. Unfortunately for me, I was famous for breaking machine needles, and consequently I had to balance them on the top of my head, which was no easy matter.

Again, should we carelessly leave anything out of its proper place, we had to wear that thing the whole of the day. On two or three occasions I have been adorned with a pail; I have had a brush and dustpan round my waist, and a large coil of clothes-line round my neck. I hope my readers will now understand a little better what is implied by the vow of poverty. This has been a short chapter, but not, I think, an unimportant one.

CHAPTER IV.

THE VOW OF CHASTITY.

THE Vow of Chastity is broken by allowing any part of the arm to be seen above the wrist, so that if we should be engaged in cleaning furniture, or scrubbing floors, or washing clothes, we are not allowed to turn up our sleeves; and as the under garments are made of coarse serge with long sleeves, which are only changed once a fortnight throughout summer and winter, the discomfort of this may easily be imagined. However, the feet may be quite bare all the year round, for those of us, at least, who were considered strong enough, as it is quite in accordance with the Vow of holy Poverty, to go without socks, stockings, or sandals.

As I was very anxious to become a saint, I gladly went about with bare feet for two winters, until I had a bad cough, and was then not allowed

The Vow of Chastity. 35

to do so any more. Often my feet were so swollen and covered with blood that I could scarcely move, but I was rather pleased at this, because the saints endured like afflictions. By saints I mean those men and women who have been canonized by the Church of Rome. To this source we went in order to find examples of how we might follow Christ. Of course our lady, the "Mother of God," as the Church of Rome calls the mother of Jesus, was always set before us as an example. Then we were in the habit of placing our holy Father St Benedict before us; then to the various saints, monks and nuns of our holy Order throughout the world we went, and again to all the saints who had been pronounced blessed by all the Popes who had ever lived.

There is one saint, "blessed John Berchmans,"[1]

[1] John Berchmans was the son of a master shoemaker named John Charles Berchmans, and was born in the year 1599. His biographers tell us that as a child he grew up as gentle and guileless as a lamb, and early shared his time between the school and the altar.

When about fifteen years of age, he joined the Society of Jesus, although his parents were somewhat opposed to his taking this step In a letter to his mother at that time he tried to bring his parents to be reconciled to his taking this who is brought prominently forward in the "Diurnal of the Soul," who particularly irritated me, because he was so perfect in every iota of his life. I used to almost wish he had been occasionally careless, or had now and again lost his temper. Whilst reading "The Monks of the West," I was quite staggered by the wholesale self-butchery several of these saints practised after their conversion.

step ; he wrote, " God is now pleased, after much prayer, out of His goodness to give me a vocation to religion and to the 'Society of Jesus,' *the hammer of all heresies, the vessel of virtue and perfection.* I hope you will not be so unreasonable as to oppose Him, but as (as I have read in history, the Egyptians offered their children to the crocodile, which they looked upon as a god, and, while it was eating them up, the parents made high festival, *so too, I hope you will rejoice as they did*, and praise God, and thank Him that your son should be found worthy," etc.

This Jesuit saint seems to have been "*celebrated for devotion to His Lord in the blessed Sacrament*" and *devotion to the Virgin Mary.* He was looked upon as a "*portent of holiness.*" He is said " *to have preserved unstained by grievous sin the white robe of baptism.*" He died in the year 1621. At eight o'clock on Friday, Aug. 13th, 1621, with "*his eyes on his crucifix,*" and with "*the holy names of Jesus* and *Mary* on his lips he went to his reward.*"

Miracles of course were said to be wrought through his relics. In 1865, Pius IX. published the decree for his beatification, and on Jan. 15th, 1888, Leo XIII., amidst the splendid festivities of his sacerdotal jubilee, solemnly canonized him as *?* saint.—EDITOR.

The Vow of Chastity.

I could never understand some of these saints. St. Benedict, in order to overcome temptations to break his Vow of Chastity, is said to have jumped into a bed of thorns and briars. I thought I would be before him, and prevent evil thoughts even presenting themselves, so I obtained permission to sting myself with stinging nettles twice a week, and continued to do so for years, though it hurt me dreadfully for two days after the operation.

A nun or novice breaks her Vow of Chastity by allowing the dress of a secular lady to brush by her sacred habit, or by raising her eyes to a lady's face when speaking to her, or by raising her eyes at any time except during the one hour's recreation. Should her brother or father come to see her, she must keep her face closely veiled from their view. Very, very seldom is she sent to speak to any other man, and then only if convent duty makes it a necessity. It was quite impossible to kiss or shake hands with any one, as we were only allowed to see visitors through a small grille, the holes of which were about an inch square, while a professed nun was always near to hear what was said. After a time the rule became stricter, and the grille was covered with a thick baize curtain, and we received orders, in addition to keeping our large thick veils down below the chin, not to draw the curtain back to speak even to a woman. It was also a great sin to speak to, or let any secular women see our faces.

I remember at one time we had a charwoman to work, and I was sent to sweep the kitchen, with orders to keep the veil low down over my face. In vain did I try to sweep, for I could not see, and dared not raise my veil. At last the poor woman tried to take the broom, saying, "Let me do it." I dared not allow this, for in so doing I should have been guilty of the sin of disobedience, and for the same reason I dared not speak. She tried hard to get the broom, and I tried hard to keep it, without speaking. At last I was almost forced to open my mouth, and I said to her, "Thank you, but I *must* do it." So I finished the work, and then in fear and trembling confessed my fault to the reverend Father. He was very angry, and made no excuse for my awkward position, but told me not to attempt to justify my conduct, and that there was no excuse for an act

The Vow of Chastity.   39

of disobedience. As a punishment, he sent me then and there to recite the whole Psalter.

Should we grow to love a sister very much, we are speedily forbidden to speak to, or hold any communication with her. This of course does not refer to our Superior, as she is in the place of God to us.

Should we put our arm around a dear young sister's neck or waist, or even take hold of her hand, such conduct would be a breach of this Vow of Chastity, and we must confess that we have been too demonstrative in our affections towards a spiritual sister. In Butler's "Lives of the Saints," we read that "St. Clare was so chaste that she would not even touch her father's hand." It was different with our Superior's hand, as it was the rule to kiss that hand when receiving the blessing.

In regard to confession, the same rules were observed as have always existed in the Church of Rome. Every thought, word, and deed had to be confessed, and we had to answer any question the priest might put to us, as nothing is wrong the priest asks in confession; at least, this is what we were told.

The priest I confessed to for the greater part of my convent life made me clearly to understand that all he said to me was for myself alone, and was not to be repeated. He bid me keep nothing back, and told me that if I did hide any known sin I should be guilty of sacrilege, my confession would be rendered invalid, and I should be putting myself in the position of Ananias and Sapphira. When I had finished my confession, he used to ask several times, "Are you sure you have told me everything?" It will thus be seen that there is no loophole or excuse to keep anything back, and I never did. Twice he asked me the most outrageous questions, which made me almost shriek, "No! Oh, no!"[1] I had been to him for some

---

[1] The late Rev. Dr. Pusey recommended Ritualistic Father Confessors to give the following advice to those Sisters of Mercy who might happen to be their penitents: "I would have great respect paid in confession to your confessor, for (to say nothing of the honour due to the priesthood) we ought to look upon them *as angels* sent by God to reconcile us to His Divine goodness; and also as His lieutenants upon earth, and therefore we owe them all reverence, even though they may *at times* betray that they are *human*, and have human infirmities, and perhaps *ask curious questions* which are not part of the confession, such as your name, what penances or virtues you practise, what are your

The Vow of Chastity.

years, and had laid my whole life open to him, and there really could be no occasion for him to put such questions to me on subjects that had never before been presented to my mind, in any shape or form. This priest is dead now, and I seldom confessed to another. After I had been a sister and under his direction for nine years, he advised me to leave that convent. Why he gave this advice, I do not know; but I replied at once that I would never go back.

temptations, etc. *I would have you answer*, although you are not obliged to do so." ("Manual for Confessors," p. 190. London, 1878.) Heaven help the poor sisters who have to answer the "curious questions" of an inquisitive or wicked Father Confessor.—EDITOR.

CHAPTER V.

THE VOW OF OBEDIENCE.

THE Vow of entire, unquestioning, and absolute Obedience renders the Superiors tyrants and their subjects slaves. A novice, or nun, must give up her will, conscience, judgment, reason, and her intellect, and must be merely a tool in her Superior's hands.[1] She may not speak to her

---

[1] The following is an extract from a lecture delivered by Mr. W. Walsh, at Bath, reported in the *English Churchman*, Nov. 26, 1886 :

"He (Mr. Walsh) had now to direct attention to the Vow of '*Obedience*,' taken by many Ritualistic Sisters of Mercy. The rule as to 'obedience' varied considerably. In *Dr. Pusey's sisterhood*, it was *very objectionable indeed.* The rule of holy obedience commands the sisters : 'Ye shall ever address the spiritual Mother with honour and respect ; avoid speaking of her among yourselves ; cherish and obey her with holy love, *without any murmur or sign of hesitation or repugnance*, but simply, cordially, and promptly obey with cheerfulness, AND BANISH FROM YOUR MIND ANY QUESTION AS TO THE WISDOM OF THE COMMAND GIVEN

The Vow of Obedience.

Superior without first prostrating her whole body to the ground, kissing the hem of her "sacred habit," and then, leave to speak being given, she may address her Superior, kneeling on both knees, with the eyes fixed on the ground. She must listen to her voice as the voice of God; for has not God addressed each nun with some such words as, "The Lord hath in His wisdom set thy Superior, and her alone, over thee, and He will only accept thy obedience through thy Superior"?

Of course we soon learnt to look upon our Superiors as possessing infallibility. In the

you. If ye fail in this, ye have failed to resist a temptation of the evil one.'

"Would not such a rule as this, Mr. Walsh continued to say, if placed in the hands of a wicked Mother Superior, lead to the most fearful results? In Father Benson's 'Religious Life Portrayed for the Use of Sisters of Mercy,' the teaching was, if possible, placed in a still more fearful light. In that book the sister is taught that—

"'A *religieuse* has made the sacrifice of her will in taking the Vow of Obedience. She is no more her own, but God's; and she must obey her Superiors for God's sake, *yielding herself as wax to be moulded unresistingly.*'"

Well did Mr. Walsh observe: "Persons who had to submit to 'obedience' such as this were as truly *slaves* as any negro."—EDITOR.

words of the Lady Prioress of Llanthony convent:

> What the Pope is to Roman Catholics, that a Superior is to a nun. *I* cannot err, in regard to you; though I may do wrong or make mistakes in regard to matters belonging to myself, yet I cannot err as regards you, for our Lord would not permit this. Therefore, no matter what I do or say to you, it must be right, so far as it concerns you; it is God's will for you, and the very slightest rebellion against my wish or orders, even in thought, is rebellion against God.

In "The Rule of our Most Holy Father St. Benedict" (Burns & Oates), on page 53, these words occur: "The third degree of humility is that a man, for the love of God, submit himself to his Superior in all obedience, imitating the Lord, of whom the apostle saith, 'He was made obedient unto death.' . . . And in order to show that we ought to be under a Superior, the word of God says, 'Thou hast placed men over our heads.'"

That this is a most extraordinary and utterly unwarranted application (?) of Scripture, I need scarcely point out to my intelligent readers.

Of course the Father Superior is as infallible as the Mother Superior; and yet I have heard the Llanthony Mother frequently criticise the reverend

The Vow of Obedience. 45

Father's doings when his actions did not exactly fall in with her ideas, or if they at all clashed with her will. This Mother, too, often accused me to the reverend Father of things I had never done. I recall to mind an occasion when I was smarting under one of these unfounded accusations, and how, in an agony of mind, I exclaimed, "It is not true, and she knows it is not true." The Father Superior commanded me to be still, and listen to God speaking to me. Practically we were taught that the Lord only reveals His will to us through our Superiors. A nun must obey the convent bell as if it were the voice of an angel. If she should be writing when the bell sounds, she must instantly lay down her pen, without even waiting to finish the formation of a letter; and as an example of how pleasing such instant obedience is to God, we were told that a certain saint was called three times whilst reciting the office of the Blessed Virgin; she obeyed promptly, and on returning and taking up her book, she found the letters written in gold;[1] and thus, even

---

[1] There must be many similar lying legends of this kind,

in this life, was her perfect obedience rewarded. When the bell rings, or a Superior calls, everything must be left at once, even though the nun knows full well she will be penanced for leaving things about, and yet she dares not stay to put them away without a breach of this Vow of Obedience.

Once I was in the "Lady Chapel," decorating the shrine, and the bell rang before I had cleared the faded flowers away. By *rule* I dared not leave them, and by *rule* I dared not clear them away, and of the two evils I chose to clear away

in order to stamp upon ignorant and superstitious minds the necessity of obedience.

In "The Secret Plan of the Jesuits," by the Abbot Leone, the following story is told : " Father Saetti, knocking at my door one morning, according to his custom, I did not open it. 'Why this delay?' he asked me. I replied that I could not open the door sooner. He then reminded me that, in all things, the most prompt obedience was the most perfect ; that, in obeying God, we must make every sacrifice, even that of a moment of time. 'One of the brethren,' he continued, 'was occupied in writing, when some one knocked at the door. He had begun to make an " O," but he did not stay to finish it. He opened the door, and on returning to his seat, he found the " O " completed, *and all in gold!* Thus you see how God rewards him who is obedient.'" Did not St. Paul prophesy that those would arise who would " speak lies in hypocrisy," and did he not say, "*Refuse profane and old wives' fables*"? (1 Tim. iv. 1-7).—EDITOR.

The Vow of Obedience. 47

the faded flowers. Soon the Lady Prioress of Llanthony came down, looked at me, and then slammed the doors, which shut me out of the nun's choir. I was afterwards reproved by the Superior, who said to me :

"Sister Agnes, if you go on in this way very much longer, you will find yourself at last where you are now, outside the doors of heaven, with the gate shut."

The truth is, a nun's obedience must be blind in its character; there must be no waiting to consider consequences, for by her vow she has renounced all claim to herself, and should the Superior command her to do what she believes to be even wrong and sinful, it is her duty to simply obey without a question, since the responsibility rests rather upon the Superior who gave the command than upon the nun who obeys it. In obeying a Superior, a nun is more sure of doing God's will than if an angel came down from heaven to give a command, seeing that Satan can transform himself into an angel of light; but there can be no possibility of mistaking the Superior's voice ! (so we were taught).

Obedience to God being the only sure road to

heaven, such obedience,[1] for a nun at least, can only be rendered pleasing and acceptable to God through the channel of her Superior; so, without strict obedience to the Superior, there can be no hope of heaven. Thus a nun must act as one who is not responsible to God for her actions! I pity the Superiors, who have not only upon them the weight of their own sins, but also that of all the nuns under their care! They have yet to learn that salvation is not the reward of man's obedience, but the free gift of God, by faith, without works.

[1] See Appendix C. for the teaching we received concerning the nature of the Vow of Obedience.—EDITOR.

CHAPTER VI.

THE DAWN OF SPIRITUAL LIGHT.

I HAD been in the convent now for some eight years, striving after perfection; but a wearisome task it was, ever striving to observe all the minutiæ of convent rules, ever confessing every little deviation from the three vows aforementioned. I had been taught that baptism had made me a child of God; that original sin had, by virtue of that rite, been taken away; but that, subsequently, if I wished to retain God's favour, I must confess every sin of omission and commission, in thought, word and deed; and that should I conceal wilfully any matter, however trivial, my eternal salvation would be endangered by any such concealment. It is perhaps difficult for those who have never been under such a hard yoke to imagine the mental torture such a system creates. I was often filled with fear lest I had not remembered *everything*, and it is no easy matter to look back through a whole life and lay everything bare before God, in the presence of a man, whom we are told to forget entirely, and think we are but repeating everything to God, who knows all beforehand, but who wills that we should come to Him in this way; and whatever shame is felt in thus opening our hearts and all its windings, must be accepted willingly as a small suffering for our sins. Sometimes a matter seems so silly or trivial that one thinks it not necessary to confess it. But the very fact of not wishing to confess it proves it to be wrong, and therefore it must be confessed. For years I went thus to confession, conscientiously and scrupulously declaring the whole of my inner and outer life. Thus did I strive to find the peace I so longed for, and I must say I did enjoy a certain satisfaction of mind until I inadvertently broke some convent rule. A sin of anger would be mortal; and had I died without confession of this sin to a priest and obtaining absolution, there would have been very little, if any, hope of my soul's salvation. I would often confess, and weep tears of real pain and bitter sorrow at my ingratitude to God, after His wonderful condescension in calling me into the "Religious Life," while so many who possibly would have grown far holier than myself were left in the world, never even having the opportunity of gaining so bright a crown, or of being so near to Jesus hereafter. I would resolve and pray that I might never do anything wrong against rule (the rule is the nun's guide to perfection, it being the only way that God intends her to reach perfection) or anything else; and to attain this perfect state, I would often spend my recreation and sleep time in making novenas to the blessed Virgin, reciting the Rosary and Litany of the blessed Virgin, or in invoking the saints; but they never seemed to answer me, and even when I redoubled my efforts, I sought their help in vain.

It was very difficult for me not to break rule sometimes, and often it would be impossible to perform obedience, as we had sometimes half a dozen obediences to fulfil at the same time, or we had some order given, and when it was accomplished, we would be severely reproved for taking upon us to dare to do such or such things; and should we try and explain our conduct, by that very explanation at least half a dozen rules were broken straightway, namely, silence broken, self-justification, answering the Superior, unwillingness to take unjust rebuke with great gratitude, etc., for all of which we had hard penances imposed. The result was that at times I was in a state of continual penance, and consequently in prolonged disgrace, whilst some sisters who were not so conscientious in confessing faults, and doing penances prescribed by rule, were deemed far holier and much higher up the ladder than myself. At last I thought myself so bad that I literally *despaired* of ever reaching perfection, or of going to heaven at all. But my Father Confessor did not think me so bad, and, in fact, he flattered me, and declared that he thought very highly of me; but this only tended to alarm me, as I thought I must be deceiving myself and him too, and I told him this, but he assured me that I must not think so, and that he felt sure I could not have such a bad opinion of myself. However, for months and months I was afraid to go to sleep lest I should awake in hell; and I was equally afraid to get up

The Dawn of Spiritual Light. 53

lest some accident should come upon me, and then I should be cast into perdition. So I was always asking to go to confession at every little fault or breach of rule.

At last the climax came, when one day the following passage from the writings of St. Alphonsus Liguori was read aloud: "A soul may yet be damned for sins which have already been confessed." How to keep silence I knew not, for I felt how terribly I had been deceived in being told that sin confessed is sin forgiven. The next day I asked leave to go to my Father Confessor, and when I was in his presence he asked me:

"Sister Agnes, have you come to confession?"

I replied, "No, I have not, for I don't believe in confession, or in anything, or anybody, or even in myself, and I scarcely believe there is a God at all."

"Dear sister, what is the matter with you? I have never seen you like this before. I always thought you very good."

Then I quoted the words of Liguori which had so upset me, and added:

"You told me that everything I confessed was

forgiven, and I believed you; but now I find it is not true."

He made at once the best explanation he could of Liguori's meaning, reconciling the words with his own apparently contradictory statement: both were right then. Be that as it may, I think that from that day I lost faith in the value and efficacy of confession, though I was obliged still to go to it.

It was just at this phase of my experience that I began to think about certain teaching that I had heard vague and indistinct rumours of; namely, that salvation was wholly the work *finished* for sinners by the Saviour's atoning blood. I had fancied that there was no truth in this, and had imagined it was some new doctrine introduced by Methodists. Finding myself in such a dilemma, I began to think a good deal about this doctrine, and at last I heartily wished it was true. But I had been so long taught that sacraments were the only sure way to heaven, that I had much to do, and after doing my utmost, I must look to Christ's work, so to speak, to supply my deficiencies, and that only when I appeared in the presence of God after this mortal life could the great question of my salvation be settled. I had so long been living under the influence of such teaching that it may be easily seen I was not very ready to accept any other form of doctrine. Yet I could not get the new idea out of my head. I somehow felt convinced of the truth of it, but I was as yet too fast bound in the old chains, and in this state of hovering between two opinions I remained for some time, until at length one night I made up my mind I would not sleep till I had settled the question between my own soul and God. The result of this decision was that I determined to lay down at the feet of Jesus all my sins, sorrows, and failings, and even my best intentions, and just to trust in His *finished* work. I thought I had actually done this, and soon fell asleep; but on awaking I felt greatly disappointed, and, kneeling down before the crucifix in my cell, I confessed to Christ how bitterly I had been disappointed in finding that in trusting in His finished work, I had not been able to find anything beyond a very momentary peace. It was whilst thus kneeling I felt—as truly I thought as it is represented in

'Pilgrim's Progress"—the whole burden of everything roll off, and a new life seemed then to thrill through me.

I had now been, as I have already said, a nun for about eight years, but my new experience did not force me out of the old routine of convent life. I quite well remember that Father Ignatius sometimes taught a doctrine very closely allied to that which I seemed lately so attracted by, but he muddled it up with a lot of teaching that seemed to contradict it. He certainly taught that all the sacramental superstructure, saint-worship, confession, etc., were only acceptable to God after we had received Christ, and thus it was that I was somehow led to believe that my new experience was right, but yet that my old life need not be set aside. I remember I was rather strengthened to continue with new vigour my self-imposed religiousness. Thus I continued, and it was only after an experience of some seventeen years that I saw that convent life—and any other life but that of the faith of the Son of God, who loved me and gave His life for me—was nothing else but a delusion.

CHAPTER VII.

LIFE AT FELTHAM CONVENT.

TEN years were passed by me at Feltham. Father Ignatius did not have very much to do with us there. The Mother, I think, used to let him know that she did not consider it a man's place to govern a number of women so entirely as he wished to do. Besides, he sometimes gave orders which she thought very indiscreet, from which great scandal might arise; and, being somewhat older than Father Ignatius, she took the liberty of representing to him, rather strongly, her views about his orders and doings. At times he would suddenly give orders from the so-called "altar," where of course no one could well remonstrate, and which would put the household arrangements out for the whole day, though he seemed to be in a great state of consternation when matters did not go forward smoothly in consequence of his orders. Sometimes, before breakfast, he would order that no one, not even the reverend Mother, should speak for a whole day, thus causing the utmost confusion, especially amongst the servants in the kitchen, who were included in the eccentric command. And yet if his own dinner was not properly cooked and served in time, he would show great displeasure. Another time I recollect how he ordered a young and delicate sister, who was very ill and consumptive, to walk bare-footed in the snow up and down the garden. On another occasion he ordered her to carry a number of stones till she had made a great heap, and then, when she had done this, he ordered her to carry them all back again ! I remember also that once he ordered a young monk, who had come to Feltham with him, to put on a high hat, and then to hop up and down the centre path in the convent garden, so that all the nuns might see him. He did this to test the young monk's humility and obedience, and to see if he was willing to become a fool for Christ's sake. The nuns did see this extraordinary sight, and exclaimed :

Life at Feltham Convent. 59

"Dear Mother, do look at Brother ——. Is he not a perfect fool?"

Nothing was too idiotic to impose in the name of holy obedience. I have seen, for instance, a brother, instead of kneeling to receive Holy Communion, standing afar off, holding up a black kettle, and at grace, in the refectory, with the muddy street door mat on his head. I have seen a sister with a handkerchief tied over her eyes, as if she was just ready for a game of blind man's buff. Remember, these follies were ordered to be done as penances, and penances were said to be special gifts of love from the Lord Jesus Christ! What profanity!

I am sure the reverend Mother had the greatest trial in Father Ignatius' freaks, or whatever they may be called; and she soon began to get sick of them, and would dread the ten days he would sometimes spend at Feltham; for she never knew what he was going to do or order next. Once he intended to bring a young monk, ill from his monastery, to be nursed by a young novice nun, and she was to devote the whole of her time to looking after him. This might have been well enough if we had been sisters of charity; but we were enclosed nuns, and were not allowed to see the face of a man, except, of course, our Superior. The Mother would not hear of such a thing, or allow the sick monk to come to the house, as she was sure it would prove an occasion of scandal. She thus set up her will and judgment to oppose Father Ignatius, and she did this on more than one occasion. But at last Father Ignatius boldly asserted that he was quite determined to have nothing but *unconditional obedience.* The Mother, and the majority of nuns in the Feltham convent, refused to accept such an unconditional obedience, and the result was that a split took place. The Mother would not sign a paper of unconditional and personal obedience, and so Father Ignatius said to those who refused : " You no longer belong to the order of the Monk Ignatius of Llanthony in the nineteenth century." However, he took with him three nuns who were ready to render the obedience he required. I was one of the three. Another of the number was the nun who took novice vows when I did. She had, however, meanwhile broken her vows, and had gone into the world for some six years, and had been a wife and mother. Her husband and child having died, she had returned to Feltham a few months before this split had taken place.

It is astonishing to contemplate how absolutely Father Ignatius required us to yield our wills to his will. Whatsoever he demanded was, he said, distinctly God's will for us, and whatsoever we did for him was God's will. To use his own oft-repeated words:

"It must be so sweet for you to wait upon your Superior, because in so doing you are really waiting upon God; in fact, in waiting upon your Superior, like Martha of old, you are waiting upon the Lord Himself."

I can assure my readers that we poor deluded nuns believed in all this; and, so far as obedience would permit, we literally vied with each other in waiting upon our Superior and preparing for him the very best we could, for we felt that nothing could be too well prepared in waiting, as we thought, upon the Lord. There was no greater penance to us than to be debarred from waiting upon his will. If any one was in disgrace for breaking rule, he would neither speak nor even look at her, nor even allow her to kiss the hem of his sacred dress!

After we had left Feltham a few weeks, Father Ignatius, and the widowed nun who had accompanied him, wrote several letters, in which the rebel nuns of Feltham were exhorted to return to their Father, by submitting to unconditional obedience. He allowed them, I think, three weeks to consider the matter; and if, at the close of that time, they remained obstinate, he would, he declared, excommunicate them, and then the awful curse of broken vows would rest upon them. The threatened curse was at length pronounced. The altar was draped in black, and an excommunication service was read through. I was greatly terrified at this most strange yet solemn act. I remember well the words that were uttered at this service:

Unless they repent of this their sin, may they be blotted out of the book of life. Amen, Amen.

Here the bell tolled. I was well nigh petrified with fear, and thought to myself, "Can all the

Feltham nuns really be under this awful curse?" At the first opportunity I asked Father Ignatius if the bell was really tolled for the Feltham Mother and nuns? He said, "Certainly it was." I exclaimed, "How awful!" He replied, "True, my child, but it had to be done." I remember how he often prophesied that the community at Feltham would only flourish like a green bay-tree for a time, and that ere long it would pass out of existence; and I must honestly confess that he did his very utmost to bring it to nought, by efforts to draw away friends and support from it. It has ever been a peculiarity of Father Ignatius to curse and excommunicate people; but those who are thus cursed only flourish all the more.

CHAPTER VIII.

CONVENT LIFE AT SLAPTON, IN DEVONSHIRE.

I WILL now pass on to say a few words about my life at the Slapton convent, in Devonshire, where we took up our abode after leaving Feltham.

We commenced life in our new home, which was part of an old chantry house, with glad, bold, and brave hearts, determined to keep the rules which were imposed upon us. Our motto was "In omnibus glorificetur Deus." We were under stricter rule than we had ever been before, but we were glad of this, as we believed we were brought nearer to Jesus the stricter the rule we kept.

I cannot say much for the peace and happiness that fell to me here after two years had passed away. During that period I was housekeeper— Mother Wereburgh sacristan, and Mother Cecilia scribe. I was greatly praised and flattered; but there was one fault found with me, and this was my unwillingness to obey implicitly the two sisters who were put above me as my Superiors. The fact is that both these nuns were jealous of me, on account of the good opinion Father Ignatius had of me. Besides, I am certain that Mother Cecilia had no right to be made Novice-mistress, nor had Mother Wereburgh right to be made Lady Prioress. The former had not been properly professed, and the latter was what is termed a "desecrated virgin," and it was unlawful, according to the constitutions of St. Benedict, for either of them to hold office. It was not right of Father Ignatius to place these women over me in the place of God, and to command me to see God in them. Although I tried hard, I could not submit to them, and thus my life became by no means a smooth or happy one.

I may mention here that, whilst residing at Slapton, a poor old woman was somehow induced to sell her little home in Herefordshire, that she might come to our convent; but alas! she "found everything," as she told me, "so different from what I expected. My life is a misery to me. I shall never believe in anything again." I must say she seemed at times somewhat peculiar; but when a person of fifty years of age begins life over again, and is expected to be as obedient as she was required to be when quite a little child, is it to be wondered at that such a return to an artificial childhood causes bewilderment? It was nothing else than devotion to Father Ignatius that caused her to give up her home.

It was the rule in choir to *hold* books; when sitting, to have the palm of each hand resting on each knee; and when kneeling, to do so perfectly upright, with hands crossed on each breast. Now this old woman had not taken any vow of obedience, and she either forgot to keep her hands in a proper position, or did not choose to do so; consequently the reverend Father, during the service, would cross the choir to her seat, and put her hands in the proper position. Five minutes afterwards she would have them clasped or folded, whereon the Father had to come to her again repeatedly. At last the poor old thing would cry and become quite hysterical. Mother Wereburgh told her she had better go home, but

Convent Life at Slapton, in Devonshire. 67

she had none to go to, for she had parted from her own home, believing that she was coming to one. Once she ran away and scandalized the nuns to the villagers. When she came back, the Mother sent for the village policeman, as she made out that the poor old woman was violent; and with the help of the policeman, she was conveyed away in the carrier's cart, and she gave the constable the money to pay her fare to her own home again.

The unkindness of the two sisters was quite sufficient to make the old woman strange and angry. I remember how she denounced these nuns, assuring them that the Lord would take vengeance on them, and it was such a speech that caused the Mother Superior to draw the policeman's attention to the alleged fact that she was mad. The simple-minded man said he could "see it." Now this policeman was made favourably disposed to the nuns, when we first went to Slapton, by the present of a leg of mutton going to his family for a Sunday dinner, and other gifts of a similar kind. The old woman was really no more mad than I am at present, but she was often made frantic with anger by the conduct of the Mother. After her return home she wrote for some clothes she had left behind at the convent, and asked the Mother to return everything that belonged to her, upon which the Mother assured Father Ignatius that she had taken all her belongings with her. Soon after this I happened to be at the linen-press with the Mother, and there I saw some of the old woman's clothes, and exclaimed, "See, here are the things she asked for!" The Mother replied, "Oh, they are only old rags." They were not. "But," said I, "are they not what she wrote for?" Three times afterwards she wrote for them, for she was badly off, having sold all her little earthly possessions to enter the "holy, happy cloister." Father Ignatius again asked the Mother to send the things off; yet in my presence she said: "I assure you, dear Father, there is nothing here of hers, and to make certain of this, I looked all through the linen cupboard the other day, and could not find a single garment belonging to her." I dared not open my lips, or even say a word to help this poor old woman to regain her clothes. They were of no value to the Mother; but once having denied that they were there, she would not acknowledge she had made a mistake, and would stick to it.

I remember too how, whilst at Slapton, an ignorant girl came to be what is called a lay-sister. She knew nothing of any kind of religion whatever, yet in a few months she made her first communion, and took novice vows for one year. I am sure she had no more idea than a new-born babe of what she had undertaken, or what was expected of her; and the hundred and one rules we had to conform to in each day were frightfully bewildering. This poor creature consequently was frequently breaking rule, and was therefore plunged in penance, disgrace and misery, and really for no fault of hers. After about two months she was sent back to the world, as she was always in trouble, especially as she was very fond of talking to the gardener, and could not see the sin of an enclosed novice talking to a man, or why she should cover her face with her veil when she wanted to see him, or any one else. As she could not make head or tail of the "glorious holy life," and was thoroughly miserable in it, she was dispensed from her vows, and sent away in a kind spirit, which was from a *prudent* motive.

I will mention the case of another young lady who came to our convent as a postulant. When she had been there a few days, she felt she had done wrong in leaving her only brother, as she had so much influence over him for good, and they were orphans. With the Mother's permission, she went back. The reverend Father was absent at the time. On his return, he sent off a letter to her, telling her that the curse of God would be upon her—that she had no faith in God. She should leave her brother in His hands, and he actually told her that she was a spiritual adulteress.

It is important that my readers should thoroughly grasp this fearful moral compulsion, which is exercised on impressible and easily influenced minds. And yet the world is told that postulants, and novices, and professed nuns, are quite free to go back if they choose. The letter of Ignatius brought this young lady back, and she was duly put to penance for leaving. She had to cover her face with a black mask, during the divine office, which is recited seven times a day and once at night. She had to sit upon the ground during the time allowed to sitting in those offices, and she was ordered to sit on the floor to eat her food. After meekly going through all her penances for the space of six weeks, she took novice vows, when her beautiful long hair was cut off quite short, in token of her renunciation of the world. She was a sweet girl of about nineteen at the time, and I know full well that she was as thoroughly miserable as she could be. When she had been a novice some time, the Lady Prioress announced to her publicly:

"Sister Ermenild, you have been a novice now over two years. Reverend Father and I both think it time you made your profession; so please to get ready to take the black veil."

Although this profession was made after we had removed to Wales, I may as well give a short account of it in this chapter.

A solemn service was performed, in which the nun was "married to Jesus Christ, Son of the most high God." A ring was placed on her finger as a token and pledge thereof, after which she was laid out on a mattress, over which was placed a black pall, ornamented with a white cross. The Burial Service from the Book of Common Prayer was then read over her, earth being solemnly dropped upon her. The *De Profundis* was sung for the repose of her soul, after which the altar was then divested of its black funeral hangings (which had been put on for this part of the service), and soon afterwards Sister Ermenild appeared in her bridal attire. She was a new creature now, raised, so to speak, to a new life. She was then led to the altar, bearing in her hands a massive lighted taper, and wearing a virgin's crown, during which proceeding a hymn was sung :

> Dead with me, then death is over,
> Dead and gone are death's dark fears.

After which came "*the cursing,*" a ceremony which is always used in the Roman Catholic Church in the consecration of a virgin, and is to the effect that—

"Should any one attempt to draw aside this present virgin, let him be cursed in his rising up and sitting down, in his standing or walking, in sleeping or waking, in eating or drinking, etc., etc., and may

Convent Life at Slapton, in Devonshire. 73

his flesh rot from his bones, and may he be blotted out of the book of life. Amen, amen, so be it."

After all this cursing was finished, the now reverend Dame Mary E. was enthroned on a seat covered with rich crimson plush, which was placed upon the altar steps, that from thence she might give all who went up to her the blessing. Father Ignatius led the way, followed by monks, boys, nuns, girls, and as many seculars as felt inclined to go. The service was then finished.[1]

---

[1] While these pages were passing through the press, the *Western Mail*, of Cardiff, on March 3rd, 1890, published a report, from the pen of its special correspondent, of the reception of three new monks at Llanthony Abbey by Father Ignatius. We reprint this report, slightly abridged :

"The great event at the morning service was the consecration of three brethren as monks. They were given new names after their consecration. The abbot gave Cymric names to the three new monks, naming one Mihangel Dewi Fair, another Catwg Fair, and the third Dyfrig Fair. The great organ thundered forth sweetest melody, and the voices of unseen choristers singing a Welsh chant ushered in the solemn service. The three monks in reply to the abbot— who was most gorgeously apparelled in cloth of gold and hood, which caught and held the lights which blazed forth from all parts of the building—who asked whether it was their wish to depart, said, 'We wish to dwell in the House of the Lord for ever!' The abbot asked, would they make a solemn vow of celibacy, obedience, and poverty. That was answered

In less than a month after, being in great trouble and disgrace with her Superior (for what

in the affirmative. After some other ceremonies of the most gorgeous description had been observed, the three brethren who sought to be made monks laid themselves down on their backs on the floor of the church. A funeral pall was placed over them to signify that they were henceforth dead to the things of this world. A long wax candle was placed at each of the four corners of the carpet on which they laid. This was followed by the Burial Service being performed by the abbot, and the great bell tolled as if for the dead, and the *De Profundis* was solemnly chanted. Moving around the prostrate figures, the abbot, now robed in black vestments, scattered ashes upon them, and said, 'Ashes to ashes, and dust to dust.' He then sprinkled holy water upon the prostrate forms. A black curtain was now drawn across the church, hiding everything from the congregation. Subsequently that was withdrawn, and it was then seen that the three monks had commenced their spiritual existence. The head of each bore the tonsure, and was encircled with a wreath as described above. The abbot received the three monks, each of whom held beneath his chin the houseling white cloth. Later on in the service the abbot, standing in wedding garments on the steps of the altar, proclaimed the three new monks as being 'the spouses of our Lord Jesus Christ,' and on the third finger of the left hand of each he placed a plain wedding ring. After the ceremony of consecration was over, the three young monks took their seats, covered with crimson cloth, and thirteen or fourteen nuns, completely concealed in white wraps, descended from somewhere, and bowed low, to receive the blessing of the monks. The above will give the reader some idea of the extraordinary and gorgeous ritual observed on the occasion."—ED.

it would be a puzzle to find out), Sister E. said to me :

"Oh! how I wish I had never taken the black veil!"

"But," said I, "you wanted to?"

She said, "No, I never asked to. You yourself heard what the reverend Mother said to me; and previous to that, she had not uttered a word on the subject."

"But," said I, "you know what the reverend Father said before every one, how eloquently he told them that the virgin about to be professed was not yet bound, and even at that last minute she was perfectly free to return to the world if she chose; but that only after she had taken this awful step she could not go back?"

To which she replied: "Yes, he did, I know, say so in public, but you do not know what he said to me in private."

Oh, how easily the world is deceived by such high-sounding phrases! "The doors are open—all are free to leave as soon as they like, etc." When people speak of inspecting convents, they should remember that to do so thoroughly, something beyond what is visible to the eye must be investigated, even the interior of each nun's heart, and the terrible moral force that has been brought to bear upon it. And remember, too, that if a sister's own mother or sister came to see her, she could not discover the deep distress that so often lies upon her daughter's heart. No nun would *dare* to tell it, even to her mother, though her heart might be breaking with misery. She would have to appear before her mother with the look of one who is perfectly happy, and even smiling, otherwise she would be instrumental in bringing disgrace and scandal upon the convent, and this, at all cost, must be avoided. I have had to appear thus, looking happy and free before my own mother, when a few minutes before I had been crying, wishing and praying that I might die.

After this digression, I will return to give an account of a novice at Slapton, who took vows on the same day as Sister E. just mentioned. They promised to let her take the black veil soon, provided only that she showed herself a submissive child (this child was over thirty), who had no wish or opinion but that of her superiors. But unfortunately for her, she had a very natural habit of forming an opinion for herself, and admitted that she thought it no harm to do so, as long as she kept that opinion to herself. But there was great harm in this (so the Superior said), inasmuch as a novice should be in all things of one mind with her Superiors, in thought, word, and deed. This novice brought with her a valuable gold watch, which she was content to give up for the time being, and, according to novice rules, she had given up her box and keys. The Mother had looked into Sister F.'s box, and there saw some things she wanted for use in the convent, and she told Sister F. so. The novice, however, was not willing that they should be used, as she had not taken life vows; in this way she first drew upon herself the Mother Superior's displeasure and censure. Shortly after this she was asked to give up her money to help in building a new cloister at Llanthony. She said she was willing to give up a part but not the whole, and would very much like to put a stone in the building. Thus by exercising her own opinion she was again brought into disgrace, and was told she could keep her money, and would not be allowed the privilege of putting a stone to the building. She must give up all her money or none. From that time she was treated with the greatest severity, and looked upon as the offscouring of all things. To make a long story short, she was soon packed off from Slapton as having no vocation to the "religious life." How strange it was that her Superiors were unable to detect this until they discovered that she was unwilling to give up her money to build a holy cloister! Before this they had a very good opinion of her.

CHAPTER IX.

CONVENT LIFE AT LLANTHONY.

I WAS looking forward to taking the black veil, but somehow the Mother had made a firm resolve to keep me, if possible, from taking this step. I may be permitted to write a few words about the present Lady Prioress of Llanthony. This lady took novice vows with me in 1869. She gained a great reputation for sanctity by an assumed air of humility, and by performing innumerable voluntary penances and antics, which put her less saintly sisters to much discomfort and disgust. I recollect her once sitting next to me in the refectory at dinner, when I saw a roasted maggot on her plate, which made me feel quite ill. I signed to her, fearing she would eat it unperceived, whereupon she at once took it upon her fork, salted it, and put it into her mouth, looking the very picture of goodness. She would of her own free will throw herself down on the floor, and meekly kiss everybody's feet, beg their prayers, and thank them for bearing with her, saying she was not worthy to be amongst us, etc. This continued until we were all perfectly sick of her, as we knew quite well by her other words and actions that she considered herself the best in the house. Sometimes she would bang her head purposely against the wall; in fact, she copied every saint, whose life she happened to be reading at the time, in his or her foolish actions, whilst if they did anything sensible, she left it out. St. Mary Magdalene of Piazzi, was her special favourite. Sister Wereburgh once planted a rotten cucumber, to see if our Lord would make it grow into a plant, which, of course, He did not, though she quite thought He would. This was in imitation of a St. Teresa, who, we read, once gave a rotten cucumber to one of her novices in order to test her obedience, desiring her to plant it in the garden. The novice obeyed without a question, when, in reward for her perfect obedience, a plant sprang from it, and bore fruit. This is one of the miracles recorded in the life of Saint Teresa. Sister Wereburgh would obtain leave to go without her dinner, and fast till tea-time, very often, but was desired to have some lunch, which would consist of dry bread. The Mother Superior at that time never asked her what lunch she had, but at last some of us found out that she had a good helping of bread and butter, and a good-sized cup of hot cocoa. She was housekeeper then, and thus had no difficulty in taking what she wanted. Thus she really had more than we did at dinner, which often consisted of two small sardines, three or four small potatoes, and half a slice of bread, thinly cut, and some water. As I do not wish to appear in the least vindictive, I will not now add more about this sister. She was the cause of distress to more persons than myself, though she managed to keep herself in favour with Father Ignatius, and became quite his model nun.

I will now tell my readers more of my experiences at Llanthony. I cannot say Father Ignatius gave us a very warm welcome to our new convent. In the first place, I remember well how dreadfully he frightened me by telling us that the place was haunted by evil spirits, as well as good. We were told by Ignatius that he had watched a whole procession of devils cross the church, while they were at matins. The brothers, we were assured, had often seen them about the house. One brother at the monastery declared that he had felt their hot breath on his cheek. This brother was a life-vowed monk, though only about twenty-one years of age. He ran away and came back so many times, that at last he said, "To prevent myself from ever returning, I shall get married," which he fulfilled by marrying an opera girl. I was told that afterwards he became a billiard-marker.

The Novice-mistress came into our room one day, saying:

"I have seen him."

"Seen whom?" we asked.

"The devil," she replied.

I was really frightened by the tales of the devils who inhabited the cloister; and to add to my terror, Father Ignatius and the Novice-mistress told me:

'Sister Agnes is SURE to see him."

I used to go about night and day, making the sign of the cross, praying to our Lord, the blessed Virgin, and to our holy Father St. Benedict, not to let me see anything, either good or evil. Sometimes I did not hear the call for the night office, and would only awake at the sound of the bell. This necessitated my going down a long dark passage alone, and returning alone to and from the church; besides, I had to stay in the church alone after matins and lauds, to recite the whole of the Lamentations of Jeremiah, as a penance for not rising when called. Not hearing was no excuse; and if we only remained in bed thirty seconds after being called, and attempted to leave the church with the others, the Novice-mistress would make signs for the sister who failed to rise, to stop and perform her penance. It used to take me a long time to do my penance, as I kept leaving off to watch for a devil.

There is supposed to be a miraculous light over the "altar," which was pointed out to us on the first day of our arrival at Llanthony. I looked for a long time, but failed to see anything but the sunshine. At last the reverend Father said:

"Do you see it, Sister Agnes?"

I replied, "No, dear Father, I do not see anything but cobwebs and sunshine."

I must not omit to write on a very distressing subject, and that is the ill-treatment I received from the Lady Prioress. After I had been about a week at Llanthony, she sent for me. On coming into her presence I knelt at her feet, and she gave me the hem of her dress to kiss. It should be remembered that we were not usually allowed to speak to the Superior without first prostrating our faces to the ground, and kissing the hem of her "holy habit."[1] But I had better give the very words of the rule: "To receive the words of our Superior, humbly kneeling, with eyes fixed on the ground." Should we break this rule, the order was "to receive any penance our Superior liked to inflict." My Superior on this occasion said,

---

[1] In the "Little Manual of Devotions," for the use of the "Pilgrims" to Llanthony Abbey, Father Ignatius teaches that—"It is a pious custom of devout Christians, on seeing a monk, to *kneel and kiss the hem of the sacred habit;* if done from love to Jesus, *and reverence to the habit* of the Consecrated Life, *a great blessing will be received*" (page 6). —EDITOR.

'Sister Agnes, you often say you wish to submit to me." I replied, "Yes, dear Mother." On which she said, " Hold your tongue, and listen to me, for now I am going to prove you; and the first thing, before I say any more, I must ask you to take off your *scapular*, for you are not fit to wear it." You, my readers, must please understand that to give up the scapular was a terrible disgrace, and it quite cut any sister off from many privileges which are highly prized, such as communion and recreation. She now imposed a severe penance upon me. I had to become *a door-mat;* that is, I had to lie prostrate in front of the church door, so that nuns, girls, monks, and boys should walk over me, and I was not allowed to get up until the last one had entered the church. I did not mind the nuns and girls treading upon me, but my nature did recoil from lying down for men to walk over me. They themselves hesitated a moment, and then deliberately walked over me. They were under obedience, and had they refused, would have incurred punishment. This penance was to last seven times a day for a week. The next penance she imposed was to make me lie prostrate on my face in front of my stall for a week during the night office, which lasts from 2 a.m. to 3.45 a.m. Then a third penance I had to undergo was to be deprived of my breakfast, and thus to go without food till 12.30 p.m. ; and when I was permitted to eat, I remember I had to take my plate and kneel before each sister, and beg food from each in turn. Though they afforded me a generous supply, I was often too ill to partake of it. After enduring two days' fasting in this fashion, the Novice-mistress begged that I might have a cup of tea, and a piece of bread at 9 a.m. She told me I must eat this, or I should become seriously ill. Ah! I did feel ill, quite wretched! but yet I longed to be quite good, pure, and holy, and this made me submit so willingly to these dreadful penances. Often at this and subsequent periods my life was such a burden to me, that I have begged and prayed that God would let me die. "O God, if you would only grant me death!" has been my prayer over and over again.

At that time I had not allowed myself to think of giving up convent life. Such a thought to me then would have been sacrilege, and the very greatest unfaithfulness to the Lord, to whom I believed myself espoused. These words which had been repeated in my ears, sounded loudly:

"Knowest thou not that the novitiate is a solemn espousal to our Lord Jesus Christ, and the consummation of the bridal tie with thy Lord will be expected of thee when thou shalt take the final vows?"

I could not forget that when I had been asked at the service of taking novice vows.

"What will become of you if you ever turn back, after taking up the golden plough?"

I had to make this reply: "I should then be unfit for the kingdom of God."

Awful words were these, words which seemed like the announcement of our own eternal damnation. Father Ignatius now says, "Why did you do these penances? You were at liberty to refuse, and leave the convent." But I would ask my readers to try and understand what *that* implied, what terrible *mental torture* (a form of torture more cruel and bitter than that imposed of old by the Inquisition) such a step involved. I am afraid no one *can* realize it who has not herself passed through it. It is a maddening kind of torture, because one is strained up to such a pitch, and made to think of the awful sin against God and one's own soul by going back; when for all eternity, by a little submission here, one would hereafter become the spotless bride of the Lamb, and gain a glorious crown to lay at His feet.

I am sure that never did any girl enter a convent, and remain in it for so many years, with a more sincere intention of serving and pleasing God through the will of her Superior than I did. I had been told many times that—

"God in His wisdom has appointed the reverend Mother, and declares that He will only accept your obedience through her, and through her alone."

And yet she was the very one that made obedience impossible, by giving me rules that were beyond my power to fulfil; and often orders were given me, which I fulfilled, and yet would after all be reprimanded severely for daring to take upon myself to do them.

After suffering much at her nands for three years, I became convinced that she would never treat me better, and I made up my mind to leave the convent. When I asked her permission to leave, she always replied, "Yes, you can go. You may go at this moment if you like." Yet she never did anything to further my departure. How could I go without clothes to put on? and I had nothing but my serge habit and cap, and was without money for my fare. Besides, it was many miles through a wild country to the nearest railway station, and I was ignorant of the way, and had been shut away from the world for sixteen years, from the early age of fifteen. The only journeys I had made were from convent to convent, and even then we had thick veils over our faces all the way, and were told not to put them up, though we were in close carriages. I wrote several times to my sister, asking her to send me some money to pay for my journey, and to tell me how to get to her, and to meet me. Over and over again I wrote to her, and received no reply. At last I discovered that my letters were not sent. Yet the world is told that nuns have *free* intercourse with their friends outside. *Nothing of the kind!*

At last I wrote another letter, and forced myself into my Superior's presence (for she had now forbidden me to go near her), and asked her to allow the letter to go by this post. I told her that it was to my sister, and that I had written for journey money, as I intended to leave. At this she quite raved, saying :

"Go out of my room this instant! I shall not allow your letter to go to your sister. You write so badly that it is a disgrace to the convent; and your other sister has written asking me not to let you write to her, as your letters worry her so."

This was not true, as my sister has since told me that she wrote to the Superior requesting her kindly to give me a few details about my mother's death. I had often written to my sister asking for a piece of my mother's hair, and it worried her so, as my darling mother was burnt to death, and there was nothing left of her but a charred coal. I had been told only that she was dead, and, very naturally, I wanted to know all about it, and continually asked for the circumstances of her death, and a piece of her hair.

The reverend Mother knew all about it, my sister having written it in the first letter announcing my mother's death, and yet she never told me what had taken place. My sister had now again written to the Superior asking her to tell me all about it, so that I should not be always asking the same question, which so worried my sister to have repeated unnecessarily as she thought.[1] My brothers, I learnt afterwards, had sent me their photographs, but they had been returned, after which they never wrote to me again, and I had meanwhile been wondering why I never heard from them.

I now felt utterly desolate to think I could not write to my sister, and I was in terror what would happen to me next: somehow I did not like to run away, as it then seemed to me dishonourable, so I said to a young sister, who I knew would report it:

"You know, I have asked over and over again to be allowed to go, and the reverend Mother will not let me. Now I am determined to watch my opportunity and run away; I shall stop at the

---

[1] At that period my letters were not kept back; but you will see that at any time that suits the Superiors letters may be and often are never sent.

first house I come to, and send some one up here to ask for money to pay my fare."

An hour after this, the Novice-mistress came with a sun-bonnet, a black and white shawl, and a sovereign, saying :

"The reverend Mother says you have asked to go so many times. Now George is going to the station, and can drive you down there to-morrow. These are all the clothes she has to give you, and that money" (putting the sovereign down on the table) "*belongs to the altar.* If you choose to do so, take it, and you are to take *nothing* away with you, not even a change of clothes."

To this I replied : "Tell the reverend Mother I cannot go out a beggar ; all I want is a change of clothes."

She sent an answer back by a new sister.

"You came to her a beggar, and you will go away a beggar."

It may be asked how it was that I felt so determined to leave. Before going on to relate how at last I did leave, I will mention that which *provoked* me to my determination. I am sure that my readers will not think it a trifling provocation.

It was as follows. One day the Mother Superior summoned us all to chapter, and commenced speaking to us thus :

" My dear children, I have come to the conclusion, which has now for some time been growing upon me (but I am now convinced of it), that poor Sister Agnes is *mad.*"

Every one seemed to start at this absurdity. I could only smile. She went on to say :

" Yes, I am quite convinced of it! and, poor child, this madness will grow upon her unless you are all very kind to her, and you all know how mad people are treated. You must never contradict them, and, therefore, you must never contradict Sister Agnes. If you do, the madness will increase ; you must just say ' yes ' to everything, unless you know she wants you to say ' no ' ; you need not take the trouble to talk to her, or put yourselves out for her, unless she asks you a question ; then simply smile at her and say ' yes.' "

She then turned to me and said :

" I forbid you to go into church at all, or to speak to any one, unless it is absolutely necessary; but of course you will do as you like about it."

My first thought was, "What a blessing! for I shall get a little peace now!" I was in peace for two days, and, if I asked questions about my work or anything, the sisters all smiled graciously, and nodded their heads, or replied, "yes." After two days had passed, I began to wonder whether I really was mad or not. This thought took such hold upon me that I would sit for hours with my head in my hands, wondering if I had really lost my reason. The thought drove sleep from me, and, in fact, was slowly driving me really mad. I asked that new sister (L——W——, from Devonshire) if she thought I was mad. She told me she did *not* think me so; but I supposed that perhaps she only said this to please and humour me, according to the instructions given by the Mother Superior. She assured me, however, that she really knew I was not mad. In spite of this assurance, my mind was in as much doubt as before, and I arrived at the conclusion that if I was not already mad, I soon should be, with this awful doubt on my mind.

I again asked leave to go, and the reverend Mother replied before them all:

"I have nowhere to send you; directly I have, you shall go."

"But," I replied, "I want to go to *my sister.*"

Turning to the chapter again, she said:

"I assure you I only keep her here out of love. She is a poor child, without a friend in the world, entirely dependent on my charity, and that of the reverend Father."

A strange suspicion was now borne into my mind, from what the Mother Superior had said about sending me away when she had a place to send me, that she was actually trying to drive me mad, and would then send me to a lunatic asylum. Hence arose my final decision to leave the convent at any cost.

To show my readers the kind of treatment I received from this lady, I will mention that one evening I was sitting alone, when suddenly I felt a great pain go through my head—so great that it almost stupified me. Then I felt a sudden box on my left ear, another on my right. I cried out, "Oh! oh!" not quite making out what it was, for the first blow had nearly stunned me.

Then a voice sounded, "I don't care if I kill

you," and I saw close to me the Lady Prioress, or the reverend Mother Mary Wereburgh of the Blessed Sacrament!

O God, Thou knowest what I write is true, without adding to it or taking aught from it; and yet I had been induced to leave my own precious mother, and had been told that the love of a *spiritual* father and mother and sister was so great, that the love of one's own parents and sisters was not to be compared to it. I always craved to be loved. I had left all my earthly relations only to gain what I was told was a higher, purer, holier, and more noble love.

Behold my reward! And such shall be yours, my reader, if you should unhappily follow in my footsteps. Yes, disappointment will follow you, bitterness of heart beyond all description, a longing to go back to those dear ones whom you have left, and yet not daring to go lest the curse of God should fall upon you. I have spent seventeen years in the cloister, and let me tell you that nearly all, or, at least, a full half of that period was one of bitter sorrow and disappointment.

It was quite a common thing to have our ears

boxed by the Lady Superior. In consequence, I became quite deaf in one ear, and, consequently, was often unable to hear the orders given me. I was reported to the reverend Father for disobedience, and I told him that it was through no fault of mine that I had failed in obeying orders, but that I had had my ears boxed to such an extent that I had become quite deaf in one ear.

One day I was coming from nones at 2.45 p.m. This "Mother" commanded me to stay where I was, and not to return to work, and then said:

"You have got the DEVIL in you, and I am going to beat him out."

All left the sacristy but myself, the Mother Superior, and one nun, who was ordered to be present at the casting out of the devil. I was commanded first to strip. I saw "the Discipline," with its seven lashes of knotted whipcord in her hand, and I knew that one lash given (or taken by oneself) was in reality seven. I should mention that at certain times it was the rule to discipline oneself.[1]

---

[1] In the *Church of England Catholic and Monastic Times* for June 24, 1884 (which was the organ of Father Ignatius),

Now my first thought when commanded to strip was, "I can't;" it would not be right or modest to strip (it meant to the waist). Then it came into my mind that Jesus did not thus think, when the soldiers ordered Him to strip to be scourged. He simply obeyed, and I felt sure that what He did I might imitate. So I said inwardly, "Yes, dear Lord, for love of Thee I can." Then I began to undress; but when I came to my vest, shame again overcame me.

"Take that thing off," said the Mother Superior. I replied, "I cannot, reverend Mother; it's too tight." The nun who was present was told to help me to get it off. A deep feeling of shame came over me at being half nude!

The Mother then ordered the nun to say the "*Miserere*," and while it was recited she lashed me several times with all her strength. I was de-

there appears an article entitled "Lent at the Monastery." It is stated that in the evening of Ash Wednesday, "Compline was said, and then, while the nuns retired to their Priory for the Service of the *Discipline*, the monks proceeded to the Discipline in the solemn choir" (page 5). This confirms the statement of Sister Mary Agnes that the "Discipline" was in use at Llanthony.—EDITOR.

termined not to utter a sound, but at last I could not restrain a smothered groan, whereat she gave me one last and cruel lash, and then ceased.

Even three weeks after she had "Disciplined" me, I had a very sore back, and it hurt me greatly to lie on it (our beds were straw put into sacks).

There was a looking-glass in the room I now occupied (nuns do not usually have them), and I looked to see if my back was marked, as it was so sore. Never shall I forget the shock it gave me. I turned quickly away, for my back was black, blue, and green all over.

I will explain to my readers what "devil" in me it was that the Lady Prioress had been attempting to drive out. You have seen how very unkind she had been to me, and, not daring to speak to her, I made a cake, which I knew her to be very fond of, and sent a note with it, begging her to be kind to me; and I told her I was willing to do anything if only she would be kind. I asked what she would have done if kindness had not been shown to her, when she asked for readmission to the Feltham convent; and I implored her, by the remembrance of that kindness which had been shown her, to be kind to me, and I signed myself, "Your loving child, M. A.," or words as near to this as I can now remember. This was the "devil" I had at this and at all other times. The fact is, that I knew too much about her, which no other sister did, and yet I never even breathed it to a soul!

Owing to the hard life we had to lead at the convent, I was not at all strong; in fact, I frequently felt ill and tired. I was often so weary that I could have laid down and willingly died. I often found it difficult to walk downstairs and up again in the middle of the night. The novice-mistress would then sometimes roughly push me, to make me go faster. I would often faint whilst reciting the Psalms aloud, and drop down on the floor, thus always hurting my head. If Father Ignatius happened to be near, they would show me some degree of kindness; but if he was away, they would drag me out of chapel and try to make me walk upstairs, or I was roughly pushed or dragged up when I had not the strength to walk. Once I remember they put me out into the sacristy, and laid me on the step of the folding door which led to the garden, and, opening the door wide, they left me there whilst they went back to prayers. I had fainted, and on recovering I would have given anything for some water, but not a drop did they give me. After a while I got so cold, and could not move myself, but, notwithstanding my pitiable condition, I had to wait till they came out of chapel. I was only partly dressed, and it was in the depth of winter. The next day I could not speak, and had a severe attack of bronchitis.[1]

It certainly was no temptation to faint, and they must have known I was not shamming, because Father Ignatius, who was always very kind in any illness, once brought Dr. Hanson to see me whilst in a faint, who said, "It comes from weakness. This young nun is very weak."

Once the Mother Superior actually pinned a large paper in front of me, and another on my back. On the latter was written in large letters: "Jesus"—"Mercy"—"Pray for me"—"Beware of me." All through that day I had to wear this,

[1] This last event, I should mention, took place in Devonshire. There are no stairs at the Llanthony convent.

and saw the partly hidden smiles, and heard the loud laugh of those about me. I did not criticize or make any objection, and tried to bear with equanimity this humiliation.

At another time she wrote a confession for me to copy, sign, and send to Father Ignatius. In this confession were these words: "I felt great repugnance to obey, when reverend Mother desired me to give up all the letters and books which reverend Father had given me." This was untrue, but holy obedience compelled me to write the untruth, and I copied the confession out, and sent it over to the monastery. In a few hours the reverend Father came over, called a chapter, and quoted what I had written as a proof that I would not submit to the reverend Mother.

"But," I said, "dear Father, I did not feel a repugnance, or let myself think anything; I obeyed at once."

"Then why did you write this note to me?"

I replied, "The reverend Mother told me to write it."

"Did you, dear Mother?" he asked.

"No!" was her answer.

I then said, "Well, she did not exactly tell me. She wrote the confession, and sent a note telling me to copy and sign it."

The reverend Father then said, "Give me her note."

I said, "I cannot, for she told me to send it back to her directly I had read it, and I did so."

He then turned to her, and she put on the most innocent face, looking at the same time aghast at me, and groaned :

"Oh!" she cried, shaking her head, as if it was too awful to listen to me. After a great deal of talking on their part, I was finally dismissed with :

"Poor child! She is not accountable for anything she says. She is quite possessed."

These words from Father Ignatius, who I thought would at last see how unjust she was to me, caused me deep grief.

This was by no means the first time I had a false confession to copy, and send as my own. Mother Cecilia (the Novice-mistress) once gave me a confession, in her writing, to copy and send to the reverend Father. I read it, and then knelt down, and kissed the hem of her dress, and said :

"I am very sorry, but I cannot write this, as it is untrue."

Her reply was, "You can do anything you are told."

I then knew that I *must* obey, and therefore I wrote at the end of the confession:

"Dear Father, this is not true, I have only copied it."

I sealed the letter, and was going to send it, but Mother Cecilia took it, read it, and severely lectured me, saying:

"You have not a spark of the spirit of obedience in you."

She often told me to do or say what was not true, and I could not, and often I used to cry and say:

"Mother mistress, I really do want to be obedient; but that is not true, and I cannot write it."

"No," she would tauntingly reply, "I know you cannot. You have plenty of sense, you are quick and clever, etc.; but there is one thing you cannot do. You cannot give up your will, you cannot do as you are told. Therefore you cannot be a nun."

The truth was, that they did not want me to

become a fully professed nun, because, as such, I should have had a voice in the community; and having been with Father Ignatius so long, I was not afraid of him, and used to speak about everything to him, and let him know what otherwise he would not have known. In order, then, to gain their own ends, they must first lower me in his eyes, and prove by all manner of intriguing that I had "no vocation." After four years they succeeded in convincing him of it, and he finally told me I had no vocation for the "religious life." He must have been very slow of discernment not to have found that out before, considering that I had been a sister for seventeen years.

I trust all this will not appear wearisome to my readers. I hope that this book will be read by many who may possibly have very little idea of what convent life is. On the surface convent life has a great attraction for some minds. When we were in Devonshire, a girl of the name of Lily W., who lived just opposite the convent, was desperately in love with it, having seen all the glitter and outside show, and heard the sweet music and singing, and having seen the bridal ceremony of Sister Ermenild taking the white veil, and observed the peaceful looks of the nuns whom she watched walking in the garden. I would observe here, that what *appears* a peaceful look is simply an attitude that *rule* drills us into. Now, Lily W. thought that convent life must be heaven upon earth. This girl came to us at Llanthony, but she received a very cold welcome. She was given plenty of hard work, was taken no notice of, and had to keep silence all day, like the professed novices and nuns, except during recreation hour. When she had been there three days, she said to me:

"Oh, dear! it is all so different from what I thought."

She spent her days and nights in sighing and crying, and seemed so miserable that I remarked to the Prioress:

"Poor Lily seems so miserable, and she is always crying and sighing, more or less, day and night."

The Prioress replied, "Serve her right; she should not have pushed herself into a hornet's nest. If people will push themselves into a hornet's nest, they must expect to be stung."

Convent Life at Llanthony. 107

Nuns have said to me more than once: "If it were not for my vows, I would not stay in the convent another day." Another has said to me:

"Alas! I often look round and think can *this* be what I gave up my beautiful home for? If ever a woman came into a convent with a sincere desire to serve God, I did."

And I am sure she spoke the truth. Afterwards she became a hard and tyrannical woman; but it was not her fault; for convent life does one of two things—it either crushes, or hardens its victims.

I assure my readers that convent life must crush every bit of self out of its victims. I was crushed by the life, and not seldom felt inclined to drown myself.

CHAPTER X.

DAILY ROUTINE AT LLANTHONY.

AT 1.45 every morning the sisters are called by the words, "Benedicamus Domino." Each sister must instantly arise, saying, "Deo gratias," then prostrate herself and kiss the floor; and after tidying herself, she must kneel upright with her back toward the bed, in silent prayer, until the first chime of the bell ceases. The nuns then form themselves into a procession, with lighted tapers in their hands, and sing as they go to church, where they remain, singing, praying, and reciting psalms, etc., until 4 a.m. They then retire to their cells, and rest until quarter to five (unless they have the lamentations of Jeremiah to recite, or it is Lent, for during that season they remain in church from 2 to 6), when they are again awakened by the same words, and have the same routine to perform. Then follows the office of

Daily Routine at Llanthony.

"Prime." If a priest is there, mass is said, or sung, after which the "Martyrology" follows, and "prayers for the faithful departed." We then remain in silent meditation until the Angelus bell is rung, when we sing the "Angelus," and then form in procession and go to spiritual reading till 8. At that hour the bell calls us to church again, when we recite the offices of Terce and Sext, and listen to a meditation. At 8.45 the "Pittance bell" rings, and we form in procession again, and go into the refectory, where we find half-a-pint of unsweetened coffee, some dry bread, potatoes rice or porridge, and salt, some of which we *must* eat, whether we are hungry or not. Many a time, like David, have we mingled our bread with weeping, and well nigh washed our bed with tears. Of course, the rule about eating this pittance of a meal did not apply to the Superiors, for they had whatever they liked, and had it whenever they liked.

At 9 o'clock the bell again rings, and we go to the Sacristy and sing, "Veni, Creator." After this the work of the day commences, and real hard work it is.

But at 12 o'clock (midday) the bell is again rung, and we go to church and sing the "Angelus," and listen to a meditation on the blessed Sacrament from St. Alphonsus Liguori, etc. We then come out of church and go to chapter, where each sister accuses herself of any fault against rule. Should a sister omit anything, or her fellow-sisters consider she has not told everything, it is their duty to say, "I accuse sister so-and-so of doing, or saying, or leaving undone, such a thing." It may be true or false, but the person accused cannot justify herself, while the sister who has accused her is praised for doing so, and is told that it wants great courage to perform such a kindness to her sister. Sometimes (more often than not) the Superior will keep the sisters there an hour or two accusing some sister, whom she has some special spite against, of faults she never committed or even thought of, and the least transgression of rule is severely punished; while want of true charity, and the Superior's temper, are highly praised as in accordance with the will of God.

Besides these daily "chapters," each day we had to write down every transgression of rule, and to

Daily Routine at Llanthony.

present the record to the Novice-mistress every Saturday morning. If she felt inclined, she would write two or three more pages of our sins, which of course she knew nothing about. Then she would pass these confessions on to the Mother Prioress, who would do a little more scribbling, and then, in turn, pass them on to the reverend Father, who would often write underneath, "Most disgraceful," and keep us away from Sunday Communion, and return our books on Monday morning to commence the same thing over again. Chapter being over, we went back to work till three, when the bell rang again for nones.

At 3.30 the dinner bell rings, and we all formed in procession, said a long grace, and then sat down to our meal, consisting of fish or eggs, vegetables, pudding, or soup, and water. On Sundays we had chicken and pudding. Flesh meat (with this exception) was not allowed except for the Superiors, who had it every day, or twice or even three times a day, except Friday.

At 4 o'clock, the "recreation" bell rings, and again we formed in procession, and recited a prayer, offering the silence of the day past to

God. And now we all must talk, even though we may have nothing to speak about. If we keep silence for five minutes, we are supposed to be in a temper, and the erring sister is told to go to her cell till she is sent for. At 5 o'clock, the bell again rings; we form in procession, and go to church, and sing Vespers and the "Angelus."

At 6 o'clock the tea bell rings. Tea consists of bread-and-butter, or jam, or treacle, and tea. At 6.30 the bell again rings for conference ("Lives of the Saints").

At 7.30 the bell rings for compline, which often lasts till 9 o'clock, for there is compline to sing, *De Profundis*, prayers for the dead, litany of the blessed Virgin, and hymn and prayers to our holy Father St. Benedict, meditation, and the closing hymn, after which we go in procession, singing "Ave, Maria," to the dormitory, when each sister, kneeling at the entrance of her cell, closes her eyes, and sings:

> Mother of Jesus, night is come,
> And wearily we fall to sleep;
> Ask Him to guard our cloister home,
> From powers of ill His flock to keep.
> Ave, Maria; Ave, Maria; Ave, Maria.

We then undress, perform our ablutions, redress, praying at each holy garment we put on; finally we lie down, making the sign of the cross, and saying, "I will lay me down in peace," etc. The "peace" is a query. It was more often "I will lay me down in sorrow," worn out in mind and body, and thus closes the peaceful, perfect, sublime, happy, holy day!

In summer the rule differs a little, and is not quite so strict. But during the season of Lent it is much stricter, and we only have the 9 o'clock pittance, and one meal at 5 o'clock, and we actually rise in the morning at 1.45, and do not rest any more till night. On Ash Wednesday we had nothing to eat or drink until six o'clock in the evening; we stayed in church practically the whole of the day. The floor of the church is strewn with ashes and cinders from the grates, and we sit on the ground in the ashes instead of in our stalls.[1] The 6 o'clock

[1] In the article on "Lent at the Monastery," which we have already quoted from the *Monastic Times*, it is stated that on Ash Wednesday, at Llanthony, "First the Superior [Father Ignatius] received the holy ashes on his tonsured head, then the monks; after this the nuns descended. . . .

meal is scarcely touched, as every one is feeling too cold and ill to eat. After compline we have to lash ourselves with the "Discipline," and then we have to go to bed unwashed, as a penance for our sins. We are not even allowed to shake the ashes out of our serge habits before retiring for the night; to do so would be to break solemn silence, so we actually sit in ashes all day, and sleep in them all night. On Good Friday we go through a somewhat similar day, but the ashes are dispensed with. Every day, over and above the divine office and prayer, continual supplication for the conversion of sinners, and for the dead, are offered, each person taking an hour's watch before the reserved Sacrament, so that the church is not left from 5 a.m. till 10 or 11 p.m.

One by one they knelt before the priest, received the ashes on their veiled heads, and disappeared behind the Great Shrine. . . . Nones, Litany, and the seven penitential Psalms were said; the latter *kneeling or lying prostrate in the ashes* in the centre of the choir."—EDITOR.

CHAPTER XI.

ILL-TREATMENT OF CHILDREN.

I RECOLLECT how a poor orphan boy at Llanthony monastery was almost always in disgrace, and had to endure the "Discipline." The lads, when doing penance, were stripped, then laid on a long table, their faces downwards, and lashed for such faults as talking in silence time, slamming doors, leaving dust about.

Another little boy, of nine or ten—motherless—his father a dipsomaniac, after being at the monastery four or five years, was turned out and sent to London, to do the best he could, with only 2s. 6d. in his pocket. Father Ignatius said Bertie was a perfect little devil. But I can assure the reader that the end of all the boys was very much like this. Sooner or later they are turned out, or else they run away. The two mothers at the Llanthony convent were constantly dropping down on the boys, when Father Ignatius was away, for breaking solemn silence, and made even the youngest of them recite the Psalms aloud, after they were tired out by the long service of compline. Very little children, I know, had constantly to go without their breakfast as a penance. I remember well two dear little children, Ada and Alice ——. They were sent to the convent by their father, a tradesman in Hereford, who doubtless thought it a great privilege to have them there. Alice was only between three and four years of age. Mother Mary Ermenild had charge of them, and she would lash them both with the "Discipline"[1]

[1] Probably few people credit what I know to be a fact, that such instruments of torture are in use in probably all monastic and conventual institutions. I have by me now a book called "Priests, Women, and Families," by J. Michelet, published in 1874 by the Protestant Evangelical Mission.

In the editor's preface to this book there are two sets of engravings of "Articles of Piety"; or, Instruments of Torture in English Convents. Under the first set of engravings, I read thus :

"Instruments of torture are *now* practised upon nuns in Romish convents in London, and in all parts of the country."

The Romish "Articles of Piety," named on the next page,

for the most trifling offences. I often found little Alice holding her arms and crying, and would say to her (if no one was near to hear me) : "What's the matter, darling?"
were bought at Little's Ecclesiastical Warehouse, 20, Cranbourne Street, and at the convent of the "Sisters of the Assumption of the Perpetual Adoration of the Blessed Sacrament." (London.)

Such instruments of torture are fitter for the worshippers of Baal, than for the worshippers of God ; and a person using them upon cattle would lay himself open to a prosecution by the "Society for the Prevention of Cruelty to Animals." Both the parties who purchased these articles are intimately known to Mr. Robert Steele, the secretary of the Protestant Evangelical Mission and Electoral Union, 5, Racquet Court, Fleet Street, E.C.

Christian reader, it is your duty to testify, on God's behalf, against the *blasphemy* and *cruelty* of Romanism. The *Maker* and *Preserver* of man is the loving *Father*, who gave His only begotten Son to die for us, and thus make atonement for our sin.

The second engraving is headed, " Iron Disciplines of the Church." There I read :

" Saint Liguori, the Doctor of the Romish Church" (and an author strongly recommended to the nuns and monks under Father Ignatius), "commends the use of *Disciplines* to the ' True Spouse of Christ,' thus :

"*Disciplines*, or *Flagellations*, are a species of mortifications strongly recommended by St. Francis of Sales, and universally adopted in religious communities of both sexes."

Then after a minute description of some fifteen of the instruments of torture, I read these words :

"Were such cruelties perpetrated upon the *heathen*, all

She would hold up her little red arms, and sob:

"Mother Ermenild gave me the 'splin" (she could not say "Discipline").

Little Ada, too, would constantly be carried to her cell, which was next to mine, and there laid on the bed, and lashed on her bare flesh by Mother Ermenild. When the child cried, she would say:

"If you don't stop that noise, I will give it to you harder."

Then another lash would come, and then another scream, after which she would say:

"Are you going to make any more noise? because I will give it to you again, if you are!"

The child would say:

"No, Mother," and would try to smother her sobs in the bed-clothes.

our *Christian* churches would resound with appeals to the sympathy of the people to come to the help of the sufferers. This would be commendable. Why, then, is the same course not adopted on behalf of nuns, who, as Rev. Pierce Connelly says, 'are not only slaves, but who are, *de facto*, by a Satanic consecration, secret prisoners for life, and may any day be put an end to, or much worse, with less risk of vengeance here in England than in Italy and Spain'?"
—Editor.

Ill-Treatment of Children.

Once, being in my cell, I heard this Mother scolding Ada dreadfully, as a naughty, wicked, disobedient little girl, for touching the ink and spilling a little (poor child! she had been trying to write a letter to her father, whom she worshipped). The Mother then made this dear child lie down, and she gave her seven lashes with the "Discipline" on her bare flesh, in all forty-nine cuts. Later in the day I went to look at the table expecting to find it spoilt, but there was only one spot of ink on it, about the size of a pea. On another occasion I heard her lashing this poor child, who shrieked so loud that I could not endure it, and I ran to her, calling out :

"Oh, you— oh, you——"

I felt so angry that I did not know what to call her ; but I was reported to the Lady Prioress, and sent for, and severely reprimanded for daring to interfere, and take a child's part, and call Mother Ermenild names for punishing and penancing the child. I was forbidden ever to speak to the children again on any pretence whatever. This was a great trial to me, for I loved the children dearly.

Now, when Mother Ermenild first came to the convent, she was a sweet and gentle girl, but she was first crushed by the life she led, and then, when power was given her, she became as hard and tyrannical as the Novice-mistress and the Dame Mary Wereburgh.

CHAPTER XII.

SOME OF THE LLANTHONY RULES, WITH ACCOMPANYING PENANCES.

RULE 1.—Never to ask for anything that is not necessary.

Penance.—To be kept without it.

Rule 2.—Never to ask for anything that is necessary a second time, unless permission to do so be granted by the Superior.

Penance.—To be kept without it.

Rule 3.—Never to hold possession of, or make use of, anything, unless given or lent by the Superior.

Penance.—To hold it up before the Blessed Sacrament for a week, at the *Magnificat.*

Rule 4.—Never to touch or look at a book, letter, or newspaper, unless holy obedience compels us to do so.

Penance.—To wear such article tied round the neck for two days.

Rule 5.—Never to look at, or speak to, a secular or extern,[1] unless commanded by holy obedience to do so.

Penance.—To confess it at once, and to repeat exactly what we have said.

Rule 6.—In speaking to a secular or extern, to do so with eyes fixed on the ground.

Penance.—To be blindfolded at each office on the following day.

Rule 7.—Never to go beyond enclosure, or the bounds permitted by holy obedience.

Penance.—To be confined to our sleeping-cell for a week.

Rule 8.—Never to speak about our Superiors to others.

Penance.—To confess it at once, and mention what we said.

Rule 9.—Never to allow criticising thoughts upon the action of a Superior to *dwell* on the mind.

Penance.—Not to be allowed to genuflect to the Blessed Sacrament for two days.

N.B.—To a nun this is an awful penance, as she has been taught that the "Body and

---

[1] An extern is a boarder, or associate.

Some of the Llanthony Rules.

Blood, Soul and Divinity" of Jesus Christ are there present in the reserved Sacrament in the tabernacle.

Rule 10.—If we have a tendency to criticise a Superior's wisdom or the correctness of any action, to believe that thereby our Lord is injured and the vocation weakened by such thoughts, since we are under our Superiors in and for the Lord, and that the Lord reveals His will only through our spiritual Father or Mother.

Rule 11.—To conceal nothing, even our most inmost thoughts, from the abbot, or abbess.

Rule 12.—Never to repeat anything said to us by our Superiors, unless commanded to do so.

Penance.—To confess it at once.

Rule 13.—Never to speak unnecessarily during "silence," and, when necessary, only while kneeling upon both knees, with the hands under the scapular, the eyes fixed on the ground, and the words we speak must be uttered in a soft whisper, "for the Lord is in His holy temple, let all the earth *keep silence* before Him."

Penance.—To recite five psalms at recreation for each breach of this rule.

Rule 14.—To obey the convent bell as the voice of an angel calling us.

Penance if late for matins.—To recite the whole of the Lamentations of Jeremiah, kneeling.

Rule 15.—Never to be late at meals, choir, dormitory, or work.

Penance.—If late at meals, to eat off the floor; if late for choir, to kneel at the door during the office; as to the rest, any penance the Superior likes to impose.

Rule 16.—Never to speak about home or our earthly relations, except to God in prayer: "Forget also thine own people, and thy father's house; so shall the King have pleasure in thy beauty."

Penance.—Any one the Superior LIKES to appoint.

Rule 17.—To be joyful and ready in our obedience.

Penance.—To confess it at once, and wear front scapular pinned over the left shoulder for two days.

Rule 18.—Never to excuse ourselves if in fault.

Penance.—To kneel in front of the altar, *holding a large crucifix* at every office, for one day.

Some of the Llanthony Rules.

Rule 19.—Never to excuse ourselves, even if unjustly accused of any fault, unless it be necessary for God's glory that the true offender should be discovered.

Penance.—Same as 18.

> N.B.—Our Superiors never did think it for God's glory that we should give any reason or explanation (so that this part of the rule is nothing else than a farce). Under this rule they would keep us on our knees for hours.

Rule 20.—To receive the words of our Superior humbly kneeling.

Penance.—Any one the Superior likes.

Rule 21.—Never to be demonstrative in our affections, even towards a spiritual sister.

Penance.—Not to be allowed to speak to such sister for any length of time our Superior likes to appoint.

Rule 22.—To zealously observe our distribution of work, and to do so wholly to the glory of God, keeping before us the memory of eternal years, our reasons for entering holy religion, and so to glorify God and benefit His holy Church.

Penance.—To lose our recreation.

Rule 23.—Never to touch food or water out of meal times.

Penance.—To wear a piece of bread tied round the neck for two days, and to go without the next meal.

Rule 24.—To keep our affections and interests perfectly detached from all things, so that our whole hearts may be given to the Lord.

Penance.—If we broke this rule by getting attached to a picture, or any other trifle, our Superiors would deprive us of it.

> N.B.—If we had anything they especially wanted, they would take it from us, as they had (so they said) noticed us breaking the rule; and of course we dared not murmur, as that would be transgressing our vow of holy poverty.

The last two of the forty-nine rules are as follows:

Rule 48.—To read over these observances each day, with the *intention* of making them known to our Superior at the close of each week.

Penance.—To write out the whole of these forty-nine observances at recreation.

Rule 49.—In confessing our breaches of these observances to state them thus, *e.g.*: "On Sunday, I transgressed observance —— by secretly feeling annoyed at being told to do such and such a thing. Jesus only.—'They shall go from strength to strength, until they all appear before God in . . .'"

These forty-nine observances (with their penances) were given to us by the abbot, and written out for us by him, with about forty-nine others. The Superiors being above the rule, there is no occasion for them to keep them, though they are very, very strict in seeing that their subjects do so, and were always dropping down on us at every nook and corner, and making out that we had broken them, when all the time we were trying our best to keep them.

We were the slaves; they were the taskmasters, and very hard ones too.

CHAPTER XIII.

OF WHAT RELIGION IS FATHER IGNATIUS?

I HAVE often been asked this question, and in some respects it is not a very easy one to answer, because Father Ignatius has such a wonderful way of being all things to all men. He has stood on the platform and preached by the side of General Booth's wife, and has joined in their processions. He has himself told me that he has gone to a Roman Catholic Dominican monastery, and was welcomed there by the monks under the designation of the "Abbot Ignatius." He has himself told us not to let poor ignorant Roman Catholics know there is any difference between us and them, as they will not know the difference unless they are told.

Whilst we were bid to read the Bible, yet we were taught to regard it as giving a clear proof that the monastic life is the highest life on earth,

Of What Religion is Father Ignatius? 129

and our Lord's example for such a life was ever put before us: we were taught that He was an enclosed monk from the age of twelve until thirty, when He commenced His public life, because there is not a word mentioned in the Bible about Him during this period. This was supposed to afford a clear proof that the life of a monk or a nun is much higher than that even of a sister of mercy.

Though we were allowed to read a non-Roman Catholic Bible, yet with regard to other books we went to Rome for them; such as: "The Life of St. Teresa," "Life of St. Gertrude,"[1] "Life of St. Mary Magdalene of Piazzi," "Life of St. Catherine of Sienna," "Life of St. Thomas Aquinas," "Life of St. Alphonsus Liguori," "Life of the Curé de Ars," "The Diurnal of the Soul," "The Glories of Mary," and "The Paradise of the Earth."

Many other books from the same source, too many to enumerate here, were given us by Father Ignatius (and truly a man is known by his books), or were read with his sanction.

He did not approve of one thing which St.

[1] See Appendix A, and B, and C, where some Romish literature used is reviewed.—EDITOR.

Thomas Aquinas taught; namely, that if a Superior should teach what is sinful or contrary to God's law, the obedience would be illicit, and the nun would not be breaking her vow if she refused to obey. Father Ignatius taught us that he himself could not command what was wrong, because he was the father and founder of the revived monastic life in the Church of England. I cannot put this matter any plainer, for I never could quite understand what he meant, but I did foolishly believe he could not tell us to do wrong, because he said so, and for no other reason whatever. Our Office Book, too, was the Roman Catholic "Benedictine Breviary," and for years the Roman Catholic "Ordinary of the Mass" was used at the altar. Lately Father Ignatius has taken a fancy to use the Sarum missal, which seems more elaborate than the Roman ritual. The High Church party is not in great favour with him, and, as a good many of them ignore him, they are put down as "namby pamby."

The nuns were and are (when there are sufficient to perform the ceremony) to be called "Nuns of the Perpetual Adoration of the Blessed

Of What Religion is Father Ignatius? 131

Sacrament." At present this perpetual adoration is, as a fact, only for certain times and great festivals. I will attempt to describe it.

The altar is for the occasion adorned with about 105 lighted candles. These are intermingled with vases of exquisite flowers. I have known them to cost £60.

The "Sacred Host" is always in the tabernacle; but on these days, when the altar is decorated out so finely, the Host is put into a Monstrance, and enthroned amidst lighted tapers, flowers, jewels, and clouds of incense, and at the sound of sweet music and singing (in Latin) bottles of Eau de Cologne are poured over the altar, to be, as he frequently said, "wasted on Jesus," like Mary's alabaster box of ointment. The tabernacle is of exquisite beauty and workmanship, with crimson velvet curtains, looped up with massive gold chains, over which is a real diamond cross. The beautiful images of angels have enough bangles hanging on their arms to set up a jeweller's shop with, and there is a piece of cloth of gold used for the Host, on which are many jewels; one small corner of the cloth alone has, I think, seventeen rings, which formerly belonged to a certain sister. The boys on this occasion are clothed in scarlet cassocks, each with a white cotta, trimmed with lace; the abbot himself appears in gorgeous apparel, as also those who assist him. The nuns used to wear long white veils down to the ground, over which were their crimson veils, used only during the adoration of the Host, with long trains. Though these are attractive-looking, yet the weight of about twelve yards of material hanging from the head is anything but pleasant, especially in hot weather; and what with wearing these veils, inhaling the incense, and singing with all one's power for two hours or more, I generally had a very bad headache.

After the service called "Exposition of the Blessed Sacrament," all leave the chapel, except the monk or nun who remains to take the watch. After this one has remained motionless in prayer for an hour, the great abbey bell (which was consecrated to and named St. Bernard) tolls five strokes, when everybody (no matter where or in what occupation) must kneel down and

Of What Religion is Father Ignatius? 133

say, "Blessed and praised at every moment be the most holy and divine Sacrament." Then some one else takes the watch before the reserved Sacrament for another hour, and this goes on all the day, which closes with the most solemn and gorgeously bewildering "Benediction of the Sacrament," more so, I verily believe, than in any Roman Catholic Church in England.

At Christmas the Bambino is the first object of worship and adoration. This Bambino is a beautiful figure of a baby, for which (I have been told) eighty guineas were paid. This figure is laid in the manger at midnight of Christmas, amid much ritual and ceremony, after which we all formed in procession, with lighted tapers, veiled in our crimson veils, to kiss the feet of the holy Child, which adoration we also performed about nine times on Christmas Day, and every day afterwards until the octave of the Epiphany, though not so frequently as on Christmas Day.[1]

[1] Father Ignatius has himself described this service in his book entitled "Brother Placidus," and records, in connection with it, a wonderful "miracle," which he declares actually occurred in his monastery. It is hard to understand how

As seculars are not allowed within the precincts of the monks' or nuns' choir, the right reverend Lord Abbot, vested in cope and mitre, holds the

any person outside a lunatic asylum can believe in such a "miracle":—
"Matins were over at five minutes before midnight. A procession quickly formed in the Refectory; and, as the hour of joy and gladness struck, the figure of the holy Child was borne in state to the crib, with lighted tapers, incense, and chanting—

> 'Ye faithful, approach ye, joyful and triumphant,
> O come ye, O come ye to Bethlehem.'

The infant figure is lying on its linen swaddling bands, in the straw; the countless tapers are flaming, amid clouds of sweetest incense, and shouts of triumph song. The little figure was charmingly life-like—the head slightly raised, the hand also lifted, as if in blessing. In due order all present approached to kiss the sacred emblems of Incarnate Love. With long, lighted tapers they approached, and kneeling down, kissed the upraised hand. First the Abbot; then Fathers Theodore, Philip, and Drostan; after them Brothers Pancras, Oswald, Ethelred, and then Placidus. How pale the fair face of the young novice looks! How his hand is trembling, as he grasps the burning taper! . . . The novice has been longing for this moment—longing to press his burning lips upon that infant hand—longing to make his adoring confession of faith in Mary's little Babe. 'O my Jesus, my King, my God, let me come and adore Thee. . . .' With words like these bursting from his heart, but all unheard by aught save Him for whom they all were uttered, Brother Placidus knelt to kiss the little hand. 'Oh! oh!' burst from the lips of the children, while the elder brothers fell baby in his lap at the grating, for the faithful laity to pay to it their adoration. If the Abbot should not be there, the Mother Superior, Mary Wereburgh (otherwise Mrs. B.——), represents the Virgin mother, robed in a cope of white satin or silk.

We were not taught to believe in the infallibility of the Pope. Father Ignatius had been to Rome and kissed the Pope's toe, and was very proud of it too. There was no need to believe much in the Pope, for Father Ignatius and the Lady Prioress were practically our two infallible Popes.

Neither were we taught the doctrine of the immaculate conception of the blessed Virgin Mary.

I think, with these two exceptions, we were identical in doctrine with the Church of Rome. And now I leave it to my readers to decide for themselves as to what is the religion of Father Ignatius.

involuntarily on their knees. Brother Placidus had kissed the holy Child, *and, as he did so, the figure became animated with life, and bowed its head, and returned the kiss, and the little hand had been laid on the novice's head.* The taper dropped from his hand, and he fell into a deep swoon, on the floor, before the shrine of the Nativity" (pages 115-118).

CHAPTER XIV.

MY DEPARTURE FROM LLANTHONY.

THE morning for my departure at last arrived. One of the first thoughts that came to me was, " I wonder if, after all, I am mad, as they tell me I am? Perhaps I am, and that is the reason for my leaving." In solitude on that morning I made a cup of tea, feeling too ill to eat, but I cut a small portion of bread and butter, in case I should want it. No one came near me. I thought I should much like to say good-bye to some one, but I dared not speak, for it was a period of solemn silence. But I still had no small attachment to the "Novice-mistress," and would have stayed in the convent had I only the assurance that I should be permitted to live in peace, for I had been a sister so long, and (strange as it may appear) the life itself had still a certain fascination for me. I did not *then*, as I do *now*, so much blame the system, but those who treated me so strangely, and often with cruelty.

At last I went into the community room, where I knew I should find the Mother-mistress. On seeing her, I approached her and put my arms round her neck, and was about to kiss her, when she shook me off as if I had been a viper. Had she spoken but one kind word then, my courage to leave might have been seriously shaken. But now hot tears rushed to my eyes. I looked straight into her face, and knew I had made no mistake. A few minutes after this she sent me a note:

DEAR CHILD,
    I could not wish you good-bye; the reverend Mother had forbidden me to do so, or even to come near you.

It was a cold, clear, bright frosty morning, when I left the monastery at 7 o'clock. I was driven down that beautiful valley, and how I enjoyed that drive! To my surprise, my conscience did not accuse me of sin in thus leaving. The morning air seemed to clear my brain, and I knew with a happy certainty that I was not mad; a feeling of peace with God seemed to fill my soul. Such a peace I had not experienced for a very, very long time—so calm, so soft and sweet, so free!

It was sixteen years and a month since I took my first journey to a convent, and I had not taken a journey since, except when we went to Devonshire, and from Devonshire to Llanthony, and then we saw nothing, being in closed carriages, and having strict orders not to raise our veils from our faces Those veils were thick and heavy, covering our faces, and reaching down far below the chin.

But I must return to my narrative. I have explained elsewhere, I think, that the Prioress would not allow any of my letters to be sent to my sister, in which I had asked for journey-money, and requested that she would meet me, and give me instructions as to my best way of finding her. None of my letters were ever sent. When I left home to go for the first time to the convent, my sister was about seventeen years of age. Since then she had married, and was living near Gloucester. Knowing so little about the world outside a convent, I fancied that if I only asked for a ticket to Gloucester, I was certain to find my sister. Accordingly, when we arrived at Llanfihangel, in

My Departure from Llanthony. 139

Wales, I booked to Gloucester. On my arrival I asked the first man I saw with a fly to drive me to the post office, as I thought my sister lived near it. Just as I was getting into the fly I thought I had better tell the driver the name of the place where my sister lived. He replied that he had never heard of such a place; so I inquired at the booking-office, and found I must take the train to a place some miles beyond Gloucester. On my arrival at this place I went outside the station (it was now dusk) and saw what seemed to me a stage-coach, and requested that I might be driven to the post office. When I told the driver the name of the place, he said he could not take me all the way there. "I will take you," he said, "as near to it as I can, and you will then have to walk a few miles farther on." My readers may imagine what a terror I was in. I began to fancy myself put down in a lonely country road, with no house near, darkness reigning, and all this experience coming to one who had been shut up in convents for so many years. What was I to do? I was frightened at every one I met, and as to a *man*, I feared the whole race. As I was thinking that my best plan would be to try and take the next train back to Wales, I saw a carriage passing near me, in which was a sweet, gentle, pale-faced lady in mourning. I ran to the carriage, and said to the lady, tears streaming down my cheeks:

"Oh, will you please take care of me for a night, for I am looking for my sister, and cannot find her?"

She said: "Dear child, you cannot come with us. Who are you?"

I replied: "I cannot tell you who I am."

I was so afraid of saying I was one of Father Ignatius's nuns, knowing that the newspapers might be full of it shortly, and that I should be bringing trouble on Ignatius, and scandal on religion.

A gentleman now came up to me and told me to be off, speaking very roughly to me. Again I appealed to the lady, assuring her I would go away and look for my sister directly the morning came, if only she would take care of me for this one night. The gentleman again told me to be off. But the lady spoke for me, saying:

"We can't leave the poor child here, like this!"

I felt grateful to her, though it seemed useless to appeal again. Just then a still, small voice seemed to whisper these words to me: "Never mind; you are my child; I will take care of you." I stopped crying at once, and, looking up to the lady, I said :

"Thank you so very much for being willing to take care of me, but never mind; I am God's child, and I know He will take care of me."

These words were hardly uttered when the gentleman said, "Jump up." I looked in surprise, and could not think where I was to jump to, but I found he wanted me to jump up and take a seat by the coachman; but I could not manage this, as I was tired, ill, and worn out, and I had scarcely tasted food for two days. The gentleman, seeing my inability, kindly assisted me, and I was taken care of until I eventually found my sister, who was glad enough to see me. But I was so frightened at every one. Directly I heard a knock at the door I used to run up to my bed-room, in case any one should see me, so strong was the force of the habit I had acquired at the convent. My sister thought it disgraceful that I should have been allowed to come out of the convent without even a change of clothes, especially so when Father Ignatius had begged my own dear mother to give me up to him for the service of God, and after working as I had done for all those years. I explained that Father Ignatius was on one of his preaching missions, and knew nothing about my leaving. She told me to write and ask for some money. Father Ignatius sent me two pounds, with which he expected me to buy clothes, to settle myself in life, to pay my journeys, and purchase any other necessaries I might require. Two pounds! Less than half of what he has paid, or allowed others to pay, to purchase one cowl for a monk to wear at meal times and in church; less than the sum he has spent to give the Prioress and Novice-mistress Christmas presents! Two pounds, after sixteen years of hard work!

I stayed with my sister about three months, until I was a little less frightened, and then went to my sister in London. I had to be provided with every article of clothing, for the habit in which I came forth from the convent I had worn for about six winters. I was naturally careful

My Departure from Llanthony. 143

and liked to make my "religious" dress last a long time. One habit I had worn for nine summers, so really I was never an expensive or extravagant nun.

At this period, my thoughts often went out to my first Mother Superior at Feltham; I longed to see her, but for some time I felt afraid to go to her or even to write, as Father Ignatius had said so much about the members of the Feltham convent being under God's curse, and had made us think that any one who held communication with them would be committing a grave sin. At last, however, I summoned sufficient courage to write and tell her that I had left Llanthony. She wrote me a most kind letter, and asked me to go and see her; this I did, and told her all my Llanthony experiences. She seemed to take it for granted that I was coming back to her, and even asked me plainly *when* I thought of taking up my abode in the community once more? I told her I had never thought of doing so. I must frankly acknowledge that I had a very deep affection for this Mother Superior, and I did not like to disappoint her, so I arranged to return, and after being there four days she allowed me to have the novice's veil, and promised that I might take the black veil in six months' time. I must confess that this Mother, in comparison with the one at Llanthony, was kindness itself. I never found at Feltham that one sister is permitted to tyrannize over another.

After I had been there about three months the reaction came. I compared the two convents, and actually (with shame I say it) was *mad* enough to think that because the Feltham rule was not strict, therefore the life could not be so perfect! Father Ignatius's sermons now seemed to come back to me word for word, especially all he had taught me on monastic obedience and the will of God. I kept thinking it all over, and could not banish it from my memory; I felt convinced that it applied to me, that I had sinned by leaving Llanthony, and was not doing God's will by remaining at Feltham. I found no rest till I had unburdened my mind to the Feltham Mother, and I then implored her to allow me to return. She thought it nothing short of infatuation, and reminded me of what I had told her of Mother Wereburgh.

However, she left me free to do what I thought best, advising me first to write to my sister, and to see her before leaving Feltham. My sister came, but she could make no impression on me, and she could not comprehend my conduct. Indeed, I must confess I could not understand it myself; for I did not want to return, yet a mysterious something seemed to draw me, and force me on against my own will. Some such experience as this occurred to the Nun of Kenmare, for on page 29 in her "Autobiography" I read: "I was to all appearances a free agent, and I was still young, I had full liberty of choice, yet I felt in some strange way, as I have often felt since, that I had no choice, that I was led or moved or influenced by some exterior power." So was it with me in my infatuation for Llanthony: I could not help myself; I seemed forced by an invisible yet very real power, which I did not pray against, and therefore yielded to.

CHAPTER XV.

AT LLANTHONY AGAIN.

IN the month of August, in the year 1885, I found my way back to Llanthony. It was dark when I arrived at the monastery, and on reaching it I seemed, for the first time, to realize all this return implied, and I now trembled at the thought of going into the convent. I walked round about the building for some time, and then looked in at the kitchen window. The first sight that came to my view was the Novice-mistress's face, and that of Mother Ermenild, whose face and eyes seemed swollen with crying. It was now 9 o'clock, and I was wondering as to the best course for me to take. I dared not go into the convent, I could not stay outside all night, and of course I did not like to go to the monastery. Of these three evils, I chose the latter, for I was not afraid of Father Ignatius. He was always very kind to me, and would not have changed, had it not been for the influence which the Mother Superior exerted over him.

To the monastery porch I went, and pulled the bell. A monk, whose face I could not see, came down, and I asked for Father Ignatius. To my surprise, I discovered that it was the reverend Father himself who was speaking to me. He was very kind, but told me I must go to the convent. I told him I was too frightened to go. He then asked me what I had come back for, if I was afraid to go to the convent. I told him that I had intended to re-enter, but when the moment came I had not the courage. He then took me into the Church, giving me the opportunity of telling him why I had gone away. He did not give me one word of blame, except about my going to Feltham, and was most kind. He then left me, and sent the Novice-mistress to me, who did not say much; but the tone of her voice seemed to send a chill through me. The day after, the reverend Father again saw me and was very kind, and told me he had given orders that I was to be treated with the greatest kindness. For some few days accordingly I was kindly treated, and soon, at my own request, I was received as a postulant. I did not object to begin the life again from the lowest step; in fact, I believed more firmly than ever that "the nun's life is the very highest and nearest to God that any human being can live on earth." It was on a Sunday that I was received back as a postulant. There were several strangers in the Lady Chapel, and a clergyman from Hereford.

On entering the church I saw on the altar steps a *funeral pall*, and the black altar hangings that are used for the dead. A cold shudder ran through me as I wondered what they were there for. At last Father Ignatius and his brother monks came in and sang the "Adoremus in æternum sanctissimum Sacramentum" ("Let us for ever adore the most holy Sacrament"). Ignatius then turned to the grille gates that divide the monks' choir from that of the seculars, and gave out that before the little ceremony, which was presently to take place, it might be advisable to give a little explanation of the cause thereof. He said:

Our dear little sister has incurred excommunication by

At Llanthony Again. 149

holding communication with excommunicated members of our Order, *i.e.*, people who have been cut off from our Society, etc., etc.

The gates were then opened, a cloth was spread, and I was told to prostrate myself upon it. The burial pall was then placed over me, and some prayers were muttered. On rising, Father Ignatius gave me the blessing, and the excommunication I had incurred was taken off me. I then went through the same postulant's service that I had gone through nearly seventeen years before. After this Father Ignatius preached a sermon, in which he highly praised me, saying that I had endured great temptations, which had caused me to leave the convent, and that he only wondered I had not left before, but that now I wished to return; and he concluded by saying, "We hold out a loving hand to her, for our dear sister has humbled herself, and she shall be exalted."

After this, I was again admitted into community, and the Lady Prioress was for a time kind to me.

On September 29th I took novice vows again, and Father Ignatius promised me, if all went well

I should receive the black veil in six months' time. It was shortly after this that Ignatius went away on one of his preaching tours, and directly he had left the Prioress made me kneel at her feet, and in her old, terrible voice inquired whether or not I intended to submit to her, etc., etc. In wonder and surprise at the sudden storm that was bursting after so long a calm, I replied: "Yes, dear Mother, indeed I do." She haughtily replied, "That's a good thing; now we shall soon see." From that moment she was just as severe as ever in her treatment of me. The more I submitted, the more tyrannical she became. She subjected me to all manner of petty insults and penances, even in the presence of little children. I soon felt convinced that it was quite useless for me to submit or even to attempt to live in the convent any longer. I could see plainly that she could never forgive me.

After a while I wrote a note to her, as I was not allowed to speak, in which, to the best of my memory, I used the following words :

If you will only let me rest in peace until Father Ignatius comes back, I will then ask his leave to go, as I am convinced you do not wish me to stay, and will never be satisfied, no matter how submissive I am. I am convinced also that if you go on treating me with such severity, I shall in reality become a lunatic, for my mind will not continue long to bear this heavy strain.

After this note she left me alone, and did not again worry me. When Father Ignatius came home a few days before Christmas, he sent for me on Christmas Eve. I went to him and said:

"Dear Father, I am very sorry, but I cannot live with reverend Mother. I do not wish to give up serving God, or to break my vows; and if you will send me to another convent, I will gladly go, or to General Booth (Ignatius was a great admirer of the Salvation Army). I don't mind where it is so that I am under obedience, and serving God."

He replied: "Well, I'll think over the matter, whether to write to Mr. Booth about you, or to write to the Abbess Bertha, and to tell her that you are a very dear child of mine, who has been with me for a great many years, but that you cannot get on with this reverend Mother, and ask her if she will take you under her charge for a time."

He spoke most kindly to me about it. I then asked him if I might come to Holy Communion on the next day (Christmas Day), to which he replied:

"Certainly not."

Later on he wished me a happy Christmas, though he must have known that my heart was nearly breaking with sorrow and disappointment. I asked no more questions about my leaving, as he had promised to do all he could for me, and I implicitly believed him, and was content to wait patiently, asking no questions, striving to do my duty, as a sister, to the best of my ability.

One evening, soon after this interview, he sent me a note commencing, "Jesus only."

"You are," he wrote, "to take your habit off to-morrow; you ought to have done so weeks ago"; and he signed it "Ignatius, of Jesus, Abbot."

This note surprised me, for I had been patiently waiting his pleasure all this time. Next morning there were not any other clothes put into my

At Llanthony Again.

cell, so I was obliged to put on the nun's dress again; but in order to show my willingness to obey, I omitted to put on my scapular. When the Novice-mistress saw me, she said:

"Go and put on your scapular at once. You ought to be ashamed of yourself, causing such a scandal in coming out like *that*."

I knelt down and kissed the hem of her holy habit, and said:

"Mother-mistress, reverend Father said——"

But she would not let me finish the sentence, and interrupted me by saying:

"I know quite well what the reverend Father said; I read the note before you, and *when* you are told to take your habit off you will do it, and not *before*. Go and put your scapular on."

I obeyed in silence, and I now knew I should have to undergo a public scene. At 12 the bell for a visit to the blessed Sacrament tolled out, after the "Angelus" was sung in Welsh. Nuns, monks, boys and girls, and seculars, were all present in the Llanthony Church. Then Ignatius spoke:

"Sister Agnes, come down to the grating."

In fear and trembling Sister Agnes obeyed. Then, in a sepulchral voice, Ignatius said:

"As in the days of old, after great long-suffering and forbearance of our loving God, His patience at last came to an end with His people, so at last, after great patience and forbearance on the part of her Superiors, they must ask Sister Agnes to take off her veil and habit, and lay them on the altar steps."

I felt this so acutely, that I sobbed aloud:

"Will you please forgive me, dear Father, for all and whatever I have done wrong."

After which, in the presence of all, I took off my veil, and laid myself down on the altar steps. When I had become somewhat calm, I realized that a trick had been played on me, and that my Superiors had made me pass through this ordeal in order to make others believe that I had been, so to speak, suddenly cut off by the will of my Superior, and not by my own free will.

In reality, I had quite of my own free will been waiting for Ignatius's sanction, and the result of his letters to Mrs. Booth and the Abbess Bertha.

At Llanthony Again.

During the above scene I reminded Ignatius of his promise to write to the Abbess Bertha, but he replied :

"Yes, but that was before I knew you were not converted,—when I thought you were a child of God."

Now I thought I had been converted some fourteen years ago, when I was made to realize so fully that Jesus Christ was my personal Saviour, and had determined, so far as I had light, " to show forth the praises of Him who had called me out of darkness into His marvellous light." Surely, I thought, had I not been converted, I could never have endured all that I had suffered during those long years of misery! And had not Ignatius taught me that I could *best* glorify Him who had washed me from my sins in His precious blood by being a true nun ? Then I believed that this was the best way of glorifying God ; but now I know that I was under a great delusion.

This scene took place on a Saturday. On Sunday Ignatius told me I must leave the convent before 7 a.m. on the following morning, giving to the reverend Mother orders to give me

£2, and to supply me with all necessary clothing. I sent this message back :

"I do not need anything at all; but will the reverend Mother please let me have the box of clothes I brought back with me."

After some hours the box was sent to me with my clothes all turned about, and with the following message :

"The reverend Mother was obliged to look over your clothes, to see what you wanted."

I found that she had put two old table napkins full of holes, in the box, two old towels full of darns, and two coarse tea cloths (which treasures I keep to this day), a petticoat ; and besides these she gave me permission to keep a new habit. I examined closely the contents of my box, and found that a dictionary, a quantity of fine linen and other things had been taken from it. I asked her for the linen, saying that I had bought it with money my brother had given me before I returned. She sent back this message :

"Tell her I have taken nothing but what belongs to me."

I imagined she meant that as I had taken the

vow of poverty, she had a right to give or retain whatever she liked. After I had taken my departure, I wrote for my things, but I never received an answer.

This was the second time I had left convent life, which had so often been described to me as "angelic." I had endured quite enough of its misery.

CHAPTER XVI.

APPARITIONS AND MIRACLES.

IT will be as well, before making the very few remarks I am able to give on the alleged "apparitions at Llanthony," that I should give my readers a few extracts from Father Ignatius's oration on the subject, which was delivered on Tuesday evening, May 5th, 1885, at, as far as I recollect, Westminster Town Hall. This oration was based professedly on Hebrews xii. 1: "Wherefore seeing we also are compassed about with so great a cloud of witnesses," etc. It would appear from this oration that Ignatius looks upon the alleged supernatural events at Llanthony as affording witness to the truth of nineteenth century Christianity. Let Ignatius tell his own story:

Apparition 1.—On Monday, the 30th of August, 1880, Brother Dunstan went as usual, at 9 o'clock, into the church to take his watch before the blessed Sacrament. He was

Apparitions and Miracles. 159

kneeling about twenty feet from the altar. At the south side of the altar there is a large window, which was not then filled with stained glass, and consequently a bright light shone upon the altar. The brother who left the watch had no communication with the sister who next came in to take her watch. She (Sister Janet) had been a schoolmistress in the neighbourhood for many years, and was now an associate of our Order.

The brother had been half an hour at his watch, when he raised his eyes and saw, in front of the tabernacle, a kind of blue mist playing. As he looked at the mist, he thought that his eyes must be affected, and he rubbed them, thinking it was an illusion; but as he still looked, the mist thickened and densified, until he saw the Monstrance, or silver vessel which contained the Host, within the tabernacle glimmering in the mist, outside the massive door of the tabernacle, which was locked. This door is of iron, nearly an inch thick. The key was in my cell, which I had not left that morning because I had been very unwell, and had had a good deal of writing to do.

The mist gradually cleared away, and then the sacred vessel containing the Host was plain before the brother's eyes, and the sunlight in the window flashed upon it. He saw this for half an hour, and, on leaving his watch, still looked upon the vision as he went out.

Sister Janet then came in to take her watch, and knelt down, as usual, at the screen in the outer church. When she looked at the altar, she saw the same appearance; but she did not dream of its being supernatural; she imagined only that the blessed Sacrament was exposed for some reason or other; but she was much astonished to find that the Host was exposed without the usual signs of reverence and devotion which we always render when we have our three expositions in the year.

We only have the Host exposed three times a year, and they are very solemn occasions; and we pay our Lord a great deal of honour during those days. On this occasion there was no light burning, there were no flowers, and the sister was consequently much astonished, knowing how particular we are in these matters of detail and reverence. Directly her watch was over at 11 o'clock she went to the monastery porch, rang the bell, and asked to see the brother who had taken the watch before her. When he came to the grating, she said: "Why has the reverend Father left the blessed Sacrament out?"

When she had explained precisely what she had seen, and Brother Dunstan knew that the tabernacle had not been opened, he at once came to my cell to tell me what had happened.

I suggested that we should go to the church. When we went in, the apparition had disappeared.

Apparition 2.—In the evening (of the same day) after vespers, the choir-boys were in the meadow playing. All at once the noise of the game was stopped, and in a very short time one of the boys came running up to my cell, soon followed by others, saying: "Father, we have seen such a beautiful spirit in the meadow." The eldest boy, who was fifteen years old, said he was certain that what they had seen was the blessed Virgin Mary—quite certain. He said that first of all, as he was waiting for his turn to run in the game, he was looking towards an old ruined hut, where there had been a farm-house, and he saw a bright light over the hedge and the figure of a woman, with hands upraised as if in blessing, and with a veil over her face, coming to him. He stood still, and was much astonished and alarmed. The figure came almost at right angles to him, and then she passed close enough even for him to see the material of the garments that she wore. The figure passed off at right angles, and stood in a bright light in a bush about fifty feet from the boy. The bush was all illumined with phosphorescent light. The figure passed through the bush, and the light was there for some little time after the form had disappeared. The rest of the boys saw and described the same appearance.

I had all the boys in the church, where I spoke solemnly to them, separately, and heard what they had to say. I told them what an unlikely story it was, and that no one would believe them; and I asked them what could have put it into their heads to think such a thing.

But they still maintained that what they had said was true.

We watched Tuesday, Wednesday, Thursday, and Friday evenings after that.

Unfortunately I had to leave Llanthony on the Saturday, being under a promise to take the duty for a clergyman in the diocese of Exeter, where we had a convent at that time; but I left strict orders that the brothers and boys should watch every night at the same time, about eight o'clock, and then write to me, telling of any experience they might have.

On Saturday night, Sept. 4th, the boys were out playing as usual, when, all at once, the same bush became illuminated with a very bright light. One boy called out, "The bush is on fire again!"

For some time they watched the light; then they ran to the monastery to call out an elder brother.

In the meantime a junior brother had come out, had

knelt down in the meadow before the illuminated bush, and had begun to say prayers and hymns. The boys were indignant because he was saying collects and hymns that had no relation to what they considered the vision to be, and they said: "Do not say those prayers, but say a 'Hail, Mary'; for we are certain it was the blessed Virgin. If we do, our Lord will perhaps let the vision appear again."

While they were discussing, the senior brother came up, and he agreed that they should begin to sing "Ave, Maria." That instant the figure flashed again, in a cloud of light, in the same place where the first boy had seen it on the Monday.

As they sang, the figure sent out rays of light, sometimes appearing behind and sometimes in front of the hedge, and sometimes coming straight towards the illuminated bush. When they said the words in the " Hail, Mary," " Blessed is the fruit of thy womb—Jesus," they saw a second figure as of a man, with only a cloth round his loins, appearing in the light, with his hands stretched out.

Father Ignatius returned from Devonshire to Llanthony on Tuesday, September the 14th, and on that night, he says, "we watched, but saw nothing." But, in the words of the oration, Ignatius thus describes the scenes of the following night:

On the 15th of September, between eight and a quarter-past eight, we watched again. It was a very close, muggy evening. There was a heavy Scotch mist descending, and the mountains were looking very dull and the sky leaden.

It was so damp that we did not go into the meadow; but Sister Janet, who was not allowed to come to the monastery door where we were standing, went into the meadow.

We were in the monastery porch. The boys were standing on the front steps; I was standing on the top step; one brother was at my left, and another brother on my right. Two farmers were behind in the back of the porch; and a gentleman visitor—an undergraduate of Keble College, Oxford, now in Holy Orders—was a little behind me to the right.

I suggested that we should sing three "Hail, Mary's," in honour of each person of the blessed Trinity. We began a "Hail, Mary" in honour of God the Father.[1] Between the "Hail, Mary's," we, all of us, expressed our amazement at some very curious flashings of light, which we saw in all directions in the meadow, like the outlines of figures. That was the impression I had . . .

I then said, "Let us sing a 'Hail, Mary,' in honour of the blessed Virgin herself;" and we began to chant the fourth "Hail, Mary."

Directly we began to do so I saw a great circle of light flash out over the whole heavens, taking in the mountains, the trees, the ruined house, the enclosure, the monastery, the gates and everything; the light flashed upon our feet, upon the steps, and upon the buildings; and from that one great circle of light, small circles bulged out, and, in the centre of the circles, stood a gigantic figure of a human being, with hands uplifted, standing sideways.

In the distance this gigantic figure appeared to be about

---

[1] I almost tremble at allowing such blasphemy as this to appear; it is too shocking.—EDITOR.

sixty feet in height; but as it descended it took the ordinary size of a human being. At the moment it struck me that a dark appearance over the head of the figure was hair, not a veil; but I am convinced from comparing notes with the others, and also from other reasons, that it was a veil which I saw over the head.

Ignatius, after mentioning that the two brothers, and Sister Janet had seen the same vision (he does not mention whether the farmers saw it), said: "From that time no further visions appeared."

Two important reasons Ignatius then gave for "our Lord" giving these apparitions.

1. "For the good of the Church of England."
2. "For the comfort of those in the outer world."

Father Ignatius, in his oration, gave an account of his sending, a few days after this memorable apparition, to each of his nuns at Slapton, in Devonshire, "pieces of a wild rhubarb leaf, which had stood up dark against the dazzling garments of the apparition, as it appeared in the bush."[1]

He then went on to describe how a certain

---

[1] I have seen this charm in the shape of a dried piece of leaf. Miss Povey has one now in her possession.—EDITOR.

Apparitions and Miracles. 165

nun at Slapton, "a middle-aged lady," who had been a cripple for thirty-eight years, was healed by applying the said charm to her diseased limb. I will give you his own account of this supposed miracle.

On Tuesday, Sept. 21st, 1880, just seven days after the last apparition had been seen, she was quivering from head to foot with pain. She was going to lie down without lifting her diseased limb with the other limb on the bed, when something told her to use the leaf, which she had put, wrapped up in an envelope, in her pocket. She took the leaf out. She took the rosary and said ten "Hail, Mary's"; and, at the end of the "Hail, Mary's," she took the piece of leaf and laid it upon these painful abscesses. The very instant the piece of withered leaf was laid upon the abscesses they closed up and the discharge ceased; her knee was loosened at the joint, her foot was on the ground, and she was cured instantaneously.

The next morning she told and showed the reverend Mother and her sister nuns the miraculous wonder of God's infinite goodness towards her; and the news quickly spread in the village.

The vicar of the parish came to the convent, and the village people rang the village bells, for they were very fond of the nuns; and, in a day or two, there was a service of thanksgiving in the Priory Chapel, for the miracle that God had wrought. There was also an account in the local papers of what had taken place.

Father Ignatius then mentions other miracles

of healing that were, he affirms, wrought by the use of the withered rhubarb leaf. The following words may be interesting to some of my readers; they appear at the close of the oration :

> To sum up, then :
> A solemn, public testimony has now been given to a most startling, supernatural phenomena, in a *Church of England monastery*, in the midst of this unbelieving, materialistic age.
> By these phenomena the mysteries of Christianity have been solemnly confirmed ; and the Word of God has received one more " *So be it.*"
> The Church of England has been supernaturally recognised as a true portion of the Catholic Church, and her Sacraments acknowledged by a miracle.
> The monastic revival, long persecuted[1] because of the two special points above alluded to, viz., the restoration of the reserved Sacrament, and the cultus of the mother of our Lord, have now received a sanction from on High, by these marvellous manifestations.
> English Churchmen have received from God a special approval for their ancient Church, in spite of her sadly isolated position.

Having thus given, in Father Ignatius's own words, an account of the alleged apparitions and

---

[1] God grant that it may never be revived, and that it will never be recognised as a part of the Church of England's machinery !—EDITOR.

Apparitions and Miracles. 167

miracles, I feel sure many will naturally ask me for my opinion of them. My opinion is simply this: I believe something was seen which Ignatius really did believe to be supernatural, but which appearance I firmly believe to have been nothing more or less than a practical joke performed by a certain young man, who never intended it to be taken for anything supernatural, in the serious manner with which it was taken.

With regard to the vision of the "Sacred Host," I simply do not believe it at all. I believe that one of them imagined it, and told the other about it in some way, and that that other was only too ready to believe it. This is my firm conviction about the matter, and I hope that as I am no longer a nun I have not only the right to have an opinion of my own, but also a right to express it.

During my sojourn at Llanthony, I never saw anything supernatural, although there were some who ofttimes tried to work my mind up to such a state, that it was with difficulty something of the kind was not forced upon my heated imagination.

I recollect a somewhat ridiculous circumstance in this direction, that occurred on the "eve" of the "anniversary of the apparition of our Lady of Llanthony."

We were watching the procession of the Shrine, and its accompanying and subsequent rites, when suddenly the reverend Mother exclaimed:

"I see something; it's moving!"

"Where?" I asked, "for I cannot see anything."

The Mother then pointed to the "Abbot's Meadow." There *was* something moving slowly, and I watched for a few moments, and then said:

"Why, it is the cow, with patches of white on her."

And so it was, as she was obliged to acknowledge. This Mother I believe often professed to see visions, and dream supernatural dreams; and I might have thought that I saw visions, but being somewhat of an inquiring and matter-of-fact turn of mind, I preferred to be very cautious, and carefully sifted everything that had any appearance of the miraculous about it. For instance, I was once kneeling at the prayer-desk before the "altar," supposing myself to be quite alone in the church; when I suddenly saw the curtains at the back of the "altar" gently moving for some time, and I wondered what this movement could mean. Then all was all quiet again, and I resumed my devotions, thinking that possibly I had only fancied it. Suddenly, behind the flowers and candlesticks, I beheld a face, and I began to tremble, and feared even to look up again; but at last I did so, and I beheld the reverend Mother, who was, I believe, engaged in dusting. Now if I had been half asleep, I might easily have imagined I had seen a vision of a departed saint; and I think the semi-darkness in which the sanctuary was enveloped, together with the soft rays of the ever-burning sanctuary lamp, can with little difficulty lead the devotee to imagine the supernatural, especially as we were always taught that on the "altar," that miracle of miracles, or rather that imposture of impostures, took place in the transubstantiation of the bread and wine, into the body, blood, soul, and divinity of the Lord Jesus Christ.

But to return to the apparitions, an account

of which I have already given, and about which I have stated shortly my opinion.

I was at Slapton, in Devonshire, at the time they took place, and therefore I only heard what the boys had told Father Ignatius.

He asked us all : " Do you believe them ? "

The other nuns said, " Yes."

Father Ignatius then said : " Do you believe them, Sister Agnes ? " I replied, " No, dear Father, of course I don't. I never believe anything the boys say."

I had a particular dislike to the monastery boys, and I had often heard from the reverend Father what lying boys some of these very ones were, and as to ——— he scarcely ever spoke the truth.

Then, as to poor Sister Janet, she was certainly very eccentric and peculiar, and when any one injured her she usually threatened to " call up the ghost " of her dead father. She once thus threatened a man, and a priest, knowing of it, disguised himself, and frightened the poor man so much, that he refused to go back to the hut where he lived. Apart from this she had her good points, and was Father Ignatius's devoted slave.

Apparitions and Miracles. 171

As you will have noticed, the reverend Father was at Slapton Convent during most of the time when the said apparitions took place, and he heard of the visions through the letters of the brother at Llanthony, and I believe he was the only brother at Llanthony at the time, and he was but a novice-monk.

Father Ignatius read the letters to us, and I hardly knew what to make of the matter; but at last the reverend Father returned and saw for himself the most marvellous and glorious vision, after which I very naturally—considering my state of mind at that period of my life—thought it must be true, which in a sense was fortunate for me, for on his next visit he again asked me if I believed in it, and I remember well I replied:

"Yes, certainly, dear Father, I do not doubt *your* word."

He then told us that he was determined that no one should stay in monastery or convent who did not believe in it.

And now a word or two about the story of the "middle-aged lady," otherwise the Novice-mistress, the account of whose miraculous cure I have already given in the words of Father Ignatius.

To begin with, that account differs somewhat from the one I can give; but as I am matter-of-*fact* in my statements, I think it best to give the facts as I know them, for I was one of the Slapton *nuns* at the time. Yes, I was a *nun* then, although life-vows had not been pronounced by me; I was what is termed a "life-vowed novice," that is, in making my vows I made them "until the time of my profession." But I have in a previous part of this book explained that novice-vows were to all intents and purposes well nigh as binding as those made in full profession. I merely give this explanation to show you the position I was in at that period when at Slapton. Father Ignatius, in his oration on the apparitions speaks of me as a nun, for, in touching upon the healing of the Novice-mistress in the Slapton Convent, he said :

"Next she told and showed her sister nuns the miraculous wonder"; *i.e.*, the withered rhubarb leaf. Now, as a matter of fact, she

Apparitions and Miracles. 173

neither told the nuns, nor showed to them this great wonder; she may have showed and told the Mother Prioress, but no one else.

The Vicar of Slapton came to celebrate, and spoke of the wondrous miracle which had taken place in our midst. (I believe this was on a Saturday, and the miracle of healing had taken place on the previous Tuesday.)

Now, certainly we had been more or less with her all this time, and yet we knew nothing about it; so when the Slapton Vicar gave his address, I was very puzzled to know what he meant.

When the celebration was over, and we had come out of the Chapel, I asked:

"What did the Vicar mean?" and I said to the Mother, "Have you really been cured Mother mistress?" (It was then that I discovered that only the Mother Prioress knew of it.)

"Yes; have you not noticed it," she replied.

I had to confess that I had *not* noticed it, and, what is more, I never did, for she still limped, and still does. In fact, I once said, "Mother mistress, is it not strange that our Lady did not quite cure you? It would have been so much nicer if she had!' She replied, "Yes, but I must be grateful for what she has done."

Now I really did then believe she had done something, but what it really was I could not make out, as I saw no difference in her whatever, In fact, many times have I seen the poor nun flushed with pain at the exertion of moving. Most probably the abscess had run its course and closed naturally just about the time when the rhubarb leaf arrived; and as to the raising of the limb which she had been unable to do for thirty-eight years, we all know how easy it is for some persons to imagine almost anything. But all I have to say is, she was about the same when I last saw her as when I first saw her; and if any one went to see her, they would see for themselves that she still limps. While she was a novice, she had a bad attack, after which a crutch was procured for her, which she used once or twice, and then went back to her old stick; but both crutch and stick had been given up long before the apparitions, though occasionally she would take the stick to go up the hill with, to the summer-house (and I often wished I had one, for it was a tiring climb). Nevertheless the stick and the crutch are now laid at the " Shrine of our Lady of Llanthony" as *"memorials of God's wonders !"*

I remember how I have looked at this stick and crutch, and thoughts passed through my mind which I need not mention.

Since I finally left the convent, I have been told that a certain young man acknowledged to a priest that he had enacted the whole of the apparition with a magic lantern, and that the priest had written to Father Ignatius, advising him not to say anything more on the subject, or else he would make known how the whole thing came about, or words to this effect. Probably the young man was the railway clerk, who witnessed the boys' excitement on the subject, for nowhere do you hear of his having seen the apparition himself. Doubtless he was too busy amusing the others. Now I do not say positively the apparitions were produced by a magic lantern, but I was told so, and I think this is the general opinion.

CHAPTER XVII.

LIBERTY.

I CANNOT but add a chapter in which I shall especially endeavour to give a word of counsel and warning to all who may in any degree be looking upon convent life, whether in the Church of England or in the Church of Rome, with a favourable eye. I may say sincerely this book has been written with this object. And if, in doing what seemed to me so bounden a duty, I have hurt the feelings of any who are mentioned in its pages, it was not with the object of doing so that I was led to speak out the truth. My prayer for them is that they may be brought out into the same liberty that I, through God's infinite mercy, am now in the enjoyment of. I can truthfully say that in doing this I have fully counted the cost, and it *has* already cost me no small amount of pain. I have spoken the truth, and I have endeavoured to do so in no vindictive manner, but in love. Distinctly this book has been written to warn all against making the terrible mistake in life that I made. Had I but listened to and obeyed my mother, her advice would have saved me from wasting (I can use no other word, though God will doubtless overrule this mistake for my own good, and for the good of others) the best and youngest years of my life, and have prevented me from enduring years of mental suffering and misery. But when I went astray on the path that seemed so attractive and pleasant, I was very young; I was but fifteen years of age, and like, I fear, so many young and inexperienced people, I was foolish, self-willed, and fancied that I was better able to judge for myself than others were to judge for me. And so I was led to deliver myself over to the tender mercies of High Church Fathers and Mothers. I was simply bewitched by their "fair speeches," high professions of sanctity, and solemn assurances of the happiness belonging to the cloistered life.

When I think of such "false prophets," I am

forcibly reminded of the words we read in 2 Timothy iii. 6:

> Of these are they that *creep into houses*, and take captive silly women, laden with sins, led away by divers lusts, *ever learning* and *never* able to come to the knowledge of the truth.

I was led by Ignatius to believe that by my action I was doing God's will, and that by leaving my home and relations I was but obeying the command of Christ to "leave all and follow Him." Was there ever such an absurdity as this? I was not called to go on a mission to the teeming millions living in heathen darkness, and take to them the Gospel of God's grace; nor yet to work amongst the heathen in our own large towns; but positively to make myself a prisoner in one particular house, to be shut up where I could engage in no Christian or even philanthropic labour, and in *such* an isolated position I was told over and over again that I could live the highest, the holiest, and the happiest life on earth, and withal, bring down to the world around me blessings and health through the merits of "holy obedience." I was taught that I could bless, and be made a blessing to others, by "telling the beads," "invoking the saints," "confessing sins to man," by "hearing mass," and by "reciting various offices." What incredible folly!

On looking back, I find how great was my delusion, and I do heartily trust that my experience of this folly may be the means of saving girls and boys, men and women, from wasting so much precious and God-given time, which it was my sad lot to lose. I sowed the seed of blind enthusiasm, and reaped the harvest of untold misery, and blighted hopes. All the high-flown promises (which I so greedily swallowed) of the joy, the glory, the peace, the happiness of the nun's life, are *false* promises and vain delusions. Certainly at one of the three convents in which I resided it was (as some of the sisters have said) "like living in a bear-garden."

I do from the depths of my heart thank God for delivering me out of the "bear-garden," and I pray that He will deliver others, and give them courage to "come out."

It needs some courage to enter, but a hundred times as much to leave. I fear in many convents, humanly speaking, it is, after full profession, almost an impossibility to do so, for, as I have said, the moral bolts and bars are even more difficult to break through than the material ones; and these latter are, especially in Roman Catholic convents, not few or easily to be broken through. During all the years spent by me in nunneries I cannot look back to *one* sister, and say I know she is happy, that she has found *true* peace and satisfaction; but I can recollect the many who were disappointed at finding the life so utterly different from what they had been led to expect.

Alas! alas! When once we have taken up the "golden plough," there is virtually no "looking back." When once we have made our choice, we must abide by it. Many I know bitterly regret that they ever put their hands to this golden or, rather, this *gilded* plough.

If nuns were only free, and not conscience-bound, they would tell the self-same, true story which I do. But alas! they dare not speak, they even scarcely dare to think for themselves. Their reason has been given up to their Superiors (do remember this), and they have no right to think anything but what their Superiors think.

It is not your place to think, but to obey.

These words were often spoken to us. And again :

A nun is always sure of doing God's will, because her Superior's voice is God's voice to her, and even should I, your Superior, tell you to tell a lie (which of course I should not), you would be committing the sin of disobedience if you did not do as you were told.

I recollect well that a certain dear young sister was told to tell what she believed to be a lie. She was in great distress about it, and went to the Mother Superior we then had, telling her that she did not know what to do, as she must either commit the sin of lying or of disobedience.

When a monk or nun is under vows, such a man or a woman is but a *tool* to be used as the owner of that tool sees fit. Individuality is sunk in the order in which such vows have been made. Practically, men and women under vows (and it matters not whether these vows are made in the established Church of England or in the alien Church of Rome) are *dead*—dead to the world, dead to father, mother, sisters, brothers and friends; above all, dead to the "still small voice" of an enlightened conscience which once had power to speak. Yes, they are *dead* in another sense of the word, for have they not, knowingly or unknowingly, committed an act of moral suicide? They are no longer responsible beings. They have given up their souls, their bodies, their wills, their consciences and reason itself into the hands of their Superiors, who from the moment those terrible vows are taken are to them in the place of God; and whatever command the Superior gives, *that* must they obey without question and blindly. And should one Superior give a sister over into the hands of another (as was the case with me), then that one must be obeyed with the same blind obedience. We were taught by the Superior:

> If the order given is sinful, that is *my* sin, and you are not responsible; but you would be guilty of greater sin in not obeying, because it would be the sin of disobedience, and God hates that sin more than any other, because it was the sin that brought death into the world, and it will bring death to your soul.

Such being the case, we may define a nunnery as a place where slaves drag on a weary existence day and night. Whilst the slave-owners do their own sweet wills, we, their slaves, must idolatrously bow down to them, kiss the hems of their holy garments, and obey without a murmur. Murmuring at our condition is most strictly forbidden.

Indeed, should the relatives or friends of a poor nun go to the convent and there hold converse with her, that conversation must be held only through a grating, and (in our case, at any rate) the nun must have her face closely veiled. And even then it would not be possible to lodge a complaint with one's relative or friend, or even with one's own mother, since another nun is usually sent to listen. Thus it is that we were often forced to appear perfectly happy, when, in truth, we were just the opposite.

I have had thus to appear when speaking to my own sister; my heart at that time was well nigh breaking. But should a nun complain, the training she has gone through would cause her to be very distressed in mind at having been unfaithful enough to bring scandal upon the so-called "religious life," and she would feel bound to confess it at once to her Mother Superior.

I should have written this account of my experiences of convent life some two years ago, had I not then feared that by doing so I should be doing more harm than good, by exposing to the outside world what a farce and sham some who make so much profession are, to say nothing of what a farce the whole system is.

But, little by little, I have become more free from the chains which held me, and I now trust that this book will do more good than harm by saving others from being led away by the power of Satan, for I believe it to be through Satanic influence that this system exists. I sincerely hope that this book will be read in the spirit in which it is written, and that thus it will be the means of saving many parents from heart-breaking separations from their beloved children.

I would ask those who are not believers in Christianity not to use it in order to bolster themselves up in their atheistical views, or to see in it a proof of the fallacy of true religion. Although I have given up convent religion, yet I am a firm believer in God. I believe that the Lord Jesus Christ died and rose again to atone for and save

His people from their sins, that the Holy Spirit can and does give to all who believe in Christ a new and a clean heart, and grace to walk in the footsteps of the Saviour.

However misguided I was when I entered in my convent life, yet I was induced to do so because I had a deep love to my Saviour, and thought I could not in a better way prove my love and increase it.

But who can be surprised at a young girl being deluded and led astray when "false prophets" arise, who *profess* so much holiness and so great and exact a knowledge of God's will?

Many there are, like myself, who have been misdirected and deceived by ritual, candles, flowers, incense, gorgeous vestments, genuflexions, sentimental music and sermons, and I know not what other nonsense. I was seeking Jesus. I asked for bread, but I was given a stone. For a time the excitement arising from convent life made me think I had found what I sought, but it was a vain delusion, as I found to my cost.

There are in English convents to-day many unhappy souls, groping in the dark. Are we to let them share my fate, and that of others, which may be worse? Nay, rather let us use our pens and voices to awaken and enlighten the men and women of England as to the truth.

Others have exposed conventual life as it exists in the Roman Catholic Church; but still the people of England can scarcely be alive to the fearfully rapid increase in the number of such convents,[1] or of the degrading and un-English and un-Christian nature of the life of a nun therein. It is not my lot to expose Roman Catholic convents; the discoveries I have made have been made in connection with the Church of England, which, alas, through the fearful growth of Ritualism, is becoming a recruiting ground for Rome.

---

[1] I believe there are now in England, Wales, and Scotland, no less than 458 Roman Catholic convents. Besides, there are about 48 houses for Jesuits, and 171 monasteries. If the people of England make no protest against this system, which is so essentially un-English, if our Government do not enforce the existing laws against the entrance of Jesuits into this country and the setting up of monasteries, and if our Government refuse to listen to the wishes of thousands in our land for convents to be impartially inspected, will not the masses, though such a course must be deplored, ere long feel almost impelled, at least with some convents, to take the law in their own hands?—EDITOR.

My opinion may not be worth much, but I hold the strong conviction that unless Protestants make a great stir, and unless the bishops of the Church set the example, England, at no very distant period, will be Romanized.

I can point to more than two or three convents in connection with the Established Church where not only Roman Catholic books are in constant use, but where the Roman Catholic Ordinary of the Mass is used, instead of our own Protestant Communion Service; and, worse than all perhaps, I know the Mass was on several occasions celebrated by a Roman Catholic priest in a Church of England convent!!

When I came out of convent life and mixed with Christian people, I discovered that the most earnest workers were those who were in the enjoyment of peace. They were living in the sunlight of God's love; they were, so to speak, good without knowing it, they had no time to be always thinking of themselves, but they were ever looking to God. Now, in the convent it had been far otherwise; we had been taught by man to try with all our might to be good according to set rules, and ceremonies, and methods handed down to us by Roman Catholic saints, or so-called Fathers of the Church, and to be continually examining and fingering our spiritual muscles to see how we were getting on in the spiritual life. In consequence of such a method, there was constant failure, as there ever will be under such a system.

I feel I have much to be thankful for that God should have led me to see my mistake in life. It was *His* work, for, in spite of the treatment I received, *I* still clung to the convent life. My motive for leaving it was mainly to get away from being misunderstood and misrepresented, and from the endurance of cruel penances. But since then my eyes have been further opened, so that I now totally disagree with the whole system, and I thank God for having so providentially taken me by the hand. He and He alone has delivered me from so many Satanic delusions, and He and He alone has made known to me the "truth as it is in Jesus," and not in Romish rites and ceremonies. I can and do indeed rejoice in the liberty wherewith Christ has made me free; I am free to serve

Him " without fear," and I am free to let my light shine that others may learn thereby to glorify my heavenly Father.

I thank Him especially for not letting me remain in the convent any longer, wasting time and precious opportunities of doing good and helping others. And I do pray that He will ever keep me in a listening and waiting attitude of mind upon Himself, so that I may " hear what the Lord will speak: for He will speak peace unto His people, and to His saints." And may He so speak to me that I may *never* " turn again to folly."

That God may use these poor efforts of mine to open the eyes of many, is the prayer of her who, with the man whose eyes the Lord once opened, can say, " Once I was blind, now I see."

DEVOTIONAL BOOKS

USED BY

SISTER MARY AGNES, O.S.B.

APPENDIX A.

"MANUAL OF DEVOTIONS TO OUR HOLY FATHER, ST. BENEDICT, ABBOT AND PATRIARCH OF THE WESTERN MONKS; TO HIS SISTER, ST. SCHOLASTICA, VIRGIN AND ABBESS; AND TO ALL SAINTS OF HIS ORDER." (London : Catholic Publishing and Bookselling Co. Limited.)

Father Ignatius calls himself a Benedictine monk, and his nuns belong to the same order. One would have supposed that though he imitated Rome in the worship of the wafer and of the Virgin, he would still have hesitated to go the full length of Romish superstition by obliging his nuns to put their trust in such questionable characters as Gregory VII., Thomas à Becket, etc. Yet on page 185 of the above book they are required to ask Gregory VII. to pray for them, and on the following page Thomas à Becket is invoked in the same manner. Who and what these two Romish saints were, truthful English history abundantly proves.

As the title of the book shows, it is intended to foster devotion to St. Benedict, to his sister Scholastica, and to all the other canonized saints of the Benedictine Order. Now, who canonized these supposed saints? Was it not Rome?

The first part is entirely devoted to the honouring and invoking of St. Benedict. Throughout this part we frequently meet with the verse, "Pray for us, O holy Father St. Benedict." There are also a number of litanies, in which he is called upon as being now "placed over the choirs of monks," as "the star of the world," as "the equal of the prophets," as "protector of his order," as "the scourge of devils," as the "Abraham of the New Testament," and is entreated with the cry, "We beseech thee to hear us." On page 47 the following invocation occurs : "Beseeching thee (holy Father St. Benedict) to be so faithfully present to me at the hour of my death, as to oppose thyself on every side where thou shalt see the assaults of the enemy most violently raging against me, that, being defended by thy presence, I may securely escape the snares of the enemy, and arrive at the joys of heaven."

Similar impieties occur throughout this and the other parts. Thus, in the part devoted to St. Scholastica, on page 131, we find the following collect : " Mercifully look down upon Thy family, we beseech Thee, O Lord, through the merits of Thy blessed Virgin, St. Scholastica ; and as by her prayers Thou didst cause the rain to descend from heaven deign, through her supplications," etc. A number of litanies also occur, in which she is addressed in the most gushing way, and asked to pray for those who thus address her.

Moreover, this book introduces prayers for the dead. Thus, on page 165, the versicle, " May the souls of the faithful departed, through the mercy of God, rest in peace."

There are many other superstitious practices contained in the book, notably the medal of St. Benedict, the wearing of which is declared on page 223 to be "a constant silent prayer to God, . . . that He would have regard to the merits of our holy Father, and for his sake would extend His own protection," etc.

Sister Mary Agnes says that the whole of this book, with the exception of the part on Indulgences, was in constant use by the nuns under Father Ignatius.

Must not then monasticism be a fostering garden of superstition, since even those who claim to reject Rome resort to the same subterfuges as Rome does to fill the void that must necessarily exist in the aching hearts of all the deluded followers of monasticism?

The next book, under Appendix B, will appear, if possible, even more grossly superstitious than the former.—(EDITOR.)

APPENDIX B.

"THE EXERCISES OF SAINT GERTRUDE, VIRGIN AND ABBESS OF THE ORDER OF ST. BENEDICT." (London: Burns & Oates.)

In the preface a short account is given of the life of St. Gertrude, which is chiefly a legendary history, and made up of some of the most absurd and ridiculous tales.

"Once, when she was pouring out her whole heart in love to its Divine Spouse, it received the impression of the five wounds of the Divine Redeemer, and Gertrude felt them continually to the moment of her death with an ever-increasing anguish and love."

Again, "On another occasion, on the Feast of Annunciation, the Mother of God fastened on her breast a heavenly jewel, wherein were seven precious stones."

Again, we have another still more extraordinary miracle vouchsafed to her; for "once she received in her heart the Divine Infant, who sprang from his crib to attach himself to her."

Must not such teaching as this be in the highest degree degrading? And must not those who can swallow such stuff be spiritually demented?

It is almost needless to point out that Saint Gertrude is said to have been devoted to the worship of the Virgin Mary. We find the following most blasphemous words on the subject: "The love of Gertrude towards Mary was in proportion to the tenderness with which the Mother of God regarded the dearest of the Spouses of her Son. Gertrude has bequeathed to us the expression of her devotion to the glorious Queen of heaven in that exquisite prayer which so expressively reveals the deep and touching character of her piety: 'Hail, fair lily of the effulgent and ever-glorious Trinity! Hail, radiant rose of heavenly fragrance, of whom the King of heaven willed to be born, and with thy milk to be fed, feed our soul with thy Divine insinuations!'" I will only give the last prayer in the book to show how the invocation of supposed saints is inculcated, as in the other book so commonly used in monastic and conventual institutions.

"O God, who hast prepared for Thyself a dwelling-place of delights in the most pure heart of the blessed Virgin Gertrude, deign, we beseech Thee, through her merits and intercession, to wipe away all stains from our hearts, that they may become meet abodes of Thy Divine Majesty, through Jesus Christ our Lord. Amen!"—(EDITOR.)

APPENDIX C.

REVIEW OF "VISITS TO THE MOST HOLY SACRAMENT AND THE BLESSED VIRGIN MARY. BY ST. ALPHONSUS LIGUORI." (Published by Burns & Oates.)

This book was sent to me by Sister Agnes, who wrote as follows when forwarding it:

"I send the book which we used daily. It was my constant friend for years; my troubles and sorrows I confided to it. The hymns with the word 'Ignatius' at the end are his, but not the others; the writing in the first part of the book, written in MS. on foreign note paper, is taken from St. Alphonsus Liguori, and *was approved of by Ignatius*, except the part I have covered over: that he did not approve of. It treats of sinful obedience. I cannot quite make it out. The book it is culled from is, I think, entitled 'The Religious Life.'"

Before reviewing the book itself, I purpose to place before you a part of the matter "written on foreign note paper," and stuck carefully into the book, acting as a kind of preface to it, as we may say.

Remember this matter is *taken from St. Alphonsus Liguori's "Life of the Religious."*

"*There is no consecration so profound, so entire as that of 'religious'* on the day of their profession, because there is *none so purifying, so constant, or so religious.* The consecration of bishops and priests is more exalted, as being a Sacrament ; it is more noble, as conferring a more sublime dignity and ineffable character ; yea, it is more powerful, because it imparts to a mere creature some of the powers of God. *But it is not so complete as the monastic* consecration, because it does not include a man's entire separation from himself and from the world ; it is not so entire, because it does not *absolutely consume the liberty*, the independence, and the spontaneousness of his nature : it is a great sacrifice and a great Sacrament, but *not a* TRUE HOLOCAUST."

I would urge my readers to stay a moment and mark carefully, and inwardly digest this description of a nun's life. Where is the liberty that is so vainly spoken of? Are we not here told that a nun by her profession has her liberty absolutely consumed ; that is to say, she is a *prisoner for life?*

Notice, I pray you, the words "it is a true holocaust." In fact, the sin of the children of Israel, who "caused their sons to pass through the fire," is committed over again. As king Manasseh "caused his children to pass through the fire in the valley of the son of Hinnom," so under the pretence of offering the nuns to the service of God, the Roman Catholics, and alas ! members of the Church of England, "sacrifice their sons and daughters to devils" (Ps. cvi. 37). It is nothing but Moloch worship over again. But to proceed with Liguori's description of the life of the religious :

" The violation of the vows is then a very grievous sin against the virtue of religion—(it is) *the crime of sacrilege.* Man, consecrated to God and to His service, *becomes something divine;* he owes himself, therefore, a religious respect, which rebounds ever to God ; and if ever he should dishonour by mortal sin the virtues of poverty, obedience, and virginity,

Appendix. 201

of which he has made profession, he would commit an outrage against the Divine honour, he would be guilty of sacrilege. What rashness! what crime! what impiety would it not be then in you to violate your vows!

"The infidelity of consecrated persons is more awful than the sacrilege committed against holy places, Eucharist vessels, holy pictures, or relics. Your soul would shudder at the mere thought of a desecrated temple, a dishonoured ciborium, a broken crucifix, or of a saint's body cast into the flames: would it then consent to far more horrible *crimes*, or to more infamous violations? Virginity derives not its nobility and worth from itself, but rather because it is an offering to the Lord, inspired and preserved by prudence and piety of the soul.

"If it should happen that a religious, in drawing comparison between his life and that of Christians in the world, should be seized with a holy fear lest he be less zealous, less pure, or less fervent than many of them, he may still find a legitimate reassurance in the thought that his actions, though they may be apparently less virtuous and brilliant, derive, notwithstanding, greater value and more real devotion than theirs from the virtue of religion, which is their chief source, and which has so high a place amongst the more virtuous."

Do we not see here how a nun is taught to meet what must be an oft-recurring thought—that her life is utterly useless, and that she is unable to devote herself actively to the service of God, and that misery and unhappiness surround her, and that she cannot be so pure as many who, living in the world, are not shut up, so to speak, with only their own heart's corruptions to brood over. She is taught that all these serious failings are more than atoned for by the mere fact that she has made a solemn profession of poverty, chastity, and obedience. But to proceed.

"He may be consoled that he has eternally consecrated to the Lord the root of his actions in such a way that they all bear the threefold character of a profound religion, ardent generosity (?), and eternal attachment to that which is good. We may reasonably suppose that on its entrance into religion, by making profession of the vows, *the Christian soul obtains remission of all its sins.* Not that the religious profession, considered in itself, possesses a sacramental virtue, operating by its own intrinsic and independent office, or that it can, like baptism and penance, blot out the stain of sin; but if it be sincere, it is a most excellent act of perfect charity, which unites us very closely to God, by an effectual outpouring of His sanctifying grace, and by an abundant remission of those temporal punishments which remain due to sin after its guilt has been forgiven.

"Before dismissing this noble subject of religious profession let us not omit to observe that the *vow of obedience is its chief feature.* That which is done by obedience is more agreeable to God than that which is performed by one's own will. Your Superior is like a sacred vessel wherein God has placed for us all His desires and graces, and the true proof of religious sanctity, the sure token of perfection, is the perfection of *obedience* to all Superiors.

"Need we add that obedience has its limits. There are, firstly, things forbidden by the *law of God,* which a Superior cannot prescribe without injustice, since, being then no longer subordinate to the Divine will, he can no longer serve as a medium between him and his subject. They are without the pale of obedience, and the Superior has no authority to enforce them. The subject, therefore, is not to act contrary

Appendix. 203

to the law of God, or to the rule which they profess to follow; in such obedience would be *illicit.*"

I must make a few observations on this matter of obedience. Notice how, by such an obedience, a professed nun (or monk) transfers to an erring mortal the whole responsibility of her actions. She has to find out God's will through the Superior's. The Superior is to her in the place of God, and practically his law and order becomes for her God's law and order. How can she remonstrate, when the Superior commands what is against the law of God, when she has been taught that she can only learn what is God's law through the medium of the Superior? And if she dared to resist her Superior's will because she felt it to be leading her astray, do you suppose that the Superior would ever acknowledge himself or herself to be in the wrong? And is it likely that the poor nun would escape some terrible penance for daring to doubt the propriety of any behest?

But the last paragraph, commencing "Need we add that obedience has its limits," and closing with "Such obedience would be illicit," was carefully hidden, for Father Ignatius had told his nuns to *paste a piece of paper over it,* since he *could not agree* with the Romish doctor! He required an absolute and unconditional obedience, and believed it impossible for a Superior to prescribe any law that was against the law of God.

St. Alphonsus Liguori has always been considered an extreme exponent of Romish doctrines; but now we find a man holding orders in the Church of England going even beyond Liguori. I beg my readers to make a special note of this. I will now finish my extracts from the writing on foreign note-paper inserted in the book I am about to review.

"The religious is a person consecrated *for ever* to the divine service" (mark this "*for ever*"—a prisoner for life, my friends, nothing more or less), "and who cannot disgrace his high dignity without committing sacrilege. He has solemnly vowed that he will belong to no other but God; he has devoted himself to follow after eternal wisdom in order to become perfect, and the religious, in sinning, has stripped himself of his justice and merits and become a shameful ruin, a horrid corpse."

(This is enough to frighten a poor, timid girl, and to bind her in chains to her prison.)

"The spiritual dangers of the religious life are not to be attributed to the vows, but rather to the fault, of him who, by changing his mind, transgresses those vows. Do not then, under the pressure of *most cruel temptations*"—(who makes them cruel? Read the experiences of Miss Povey or any other nun who has had the good fortune to escape, or to be turned out of her prison, and you will find out)—"regret the profession you have made in the *fulness of liberty*"—(remember that previous to profession the Superiors have cunningly woven their entangling web around the nun, and the profession may be compared to the spider, after he has secured his prey, *carrying the poor helpless fly* into the inner precincts of his home)—"but rather behave the more diligently to subject your impatient nature to so *salutary* a yoke." Mark the word "salutary." Is it not a well-attested fact that many nuns go mad from the unnatural confinement within convent walls?

I can only hope to give a very short review of this book, which was placed in the hands of a nun who was a member of the Church of England. I have not time for an elaborate or lengthy account of its contents. I do not think that it was only at Llanthony that this book was used, and it is to be feared that whilst the Feltham convent is now no longer under the wing of Father Ignatius, yet that, with the exception of unconditional obedience, the teaching there is as extreme and as Romish as at Llanthony, and yet I believe a clergyman, holding a licence to officiate in the diocese of London, acts as chaplain there. How long our bishops are going to allow and wink at this state of things, I know not! May God raise up many faithful men who will demand that the laws of our Protestant Church be complied with!

The above work is one of the so-called devotional books prescribed by Father Ignatius, to be used by the nuns under his control.

It is a Roman Catholic publication, in constant use in all the monastic and other institutions of that Church; was composed in Italian by Liguori, the founder of the Redemptorist Order, translated into English by the Rev. R. A. Coffin, a member of that order, and published by Burns & Oates, the leading Romish publishers in Great Britain.

The nature of this book may be readily ascertained from the fact that it presupposes the consecrated wafer to be really and truly Christ himself, and that it insists upon the Virgin Mary as being the Saviour of every one that is saved. For, in the beginning of the introduction, Liguori says:

"Our holy faith teaches us, and we are bound to believe, that in the consecrated host Jesus Christ is really present under the species of bread"; and, further on, speaking of the visits to the Virgin, he says:

"The opinion of St. Bernard is well known and generally believed. It is that God dispenses no graces otherwise than through the hands of Mary. . . . Hence, Father Suarez declares that it is now the sentiment of the universal Church that 'the intercession of Mary is not only useful, but even necessary to obtain graces,'" and he concludes :

"Do you then be also careful to always join to your daily visit to the most blessed Sacrament a visit to the most holy Virgin Mary in some church, or at least before a devout image of her in your own house."

Hence on page 25 we find a prayer to the Virgin, beginning with the words :

"Most holy immaculate Virgin, and my mother 'Mary,'" in which she is styled the "queen of the world," "the hope, the refuge of sinners," and the following blasphemous expressions are used :

"I worship thee, O great queen, and I thank thee for all the graces which thou hast hitherto granted me ; and especially I thank thee for having delivered me from hell, which I have so often deserved. . . . I place all my hopes in thee, and I confide my salvation to thy care, etc."

Hence throughout the book occur such expressions as the following :

"Sole refuge of sinners, have mercy on me." "O Mary, grant me the grace always to have recourse to thee." ".Hail, our hope." "My hope, help me." "Therefore, my lady, and my hope, if thou dost not help me, I am lost." "All who are saved obtain salvation through thee ; thou then, O Mary, hast to save me," and the like.

Extracts might be piled upon extracts, but enough have been given to show the nature and tendency of the book. Yet this book the nuns, under Father Ignatius's jurisdiction, are induced to keep as a constant companion.

It does not seem necessary to say anything further on the

head of this book: for its antichristian nature must be apparent to all students of the pure word of God. In Christ alone is salvation, and He alone is our Mediator between God and man.—(EDITOR.)

27, Paternoster Row, London,
May 1890.

HODDER & STOUGHTON'S
New and Recent Publications.

THE CHRISTIAN MINISTRY: Its Origin, Constitution, Nature, and Work. The Donnellan Lectures for 1888, together with Notes and Appendices.
By the Very Rev. WILLIAM LEFROY, D.D., Dean of Norwich (sometime Incumbent of St. Andrew's, Liverpool ; Honorary Canon of Liverpool Cathedral, and Archdeacon of Warrington). In one volume, 8vo, price 14s.

STUDIES ON THE EPISTLES. By the Rev. Professor F. GODET, D.D. Translated by Mrs. ANNIE HARWOOD HOLMDEN. Crown 8vo, cloth, 7s. 6d.

PERSONAL AND FAMILY GLIMPSES OF REMARKABLE PEOPLE.
By the Venerable Archdeacon E. W. WHATELY, M.A., late Chancellor of St. Patrick's and Rector of Werbergh, Dublin. Crown 8vo, cloth, price 6s. 6d.

IMAGO CHRISTI: The Example of Jesus Christ. By the Rev. JAMES STALKER, M.A., Author of "The Life of Jesus Christ," "The Life of St. Paul," etc. Crown 8vo, cloth, price 5s.

IRELAND AND THE ANGLO-NORMAN CHURCH: A History of Ireland and Irish Christianity from the Anglo-Norman Conquest to the Dawn of the Reformation.
By the Rev. G. T. STOKES, D.D., Professor of Ecclesiastical History in the University of Dublin, and Vicar of All Saints', Blackrock; Author of "Ireland and the Celtic Church," etc. Crown 8vo, cloth, price 9s.

BENJAMIN HELLIER: His Life and Teaching. A Biographical Sketch, with Extracts from his Letters, Sermons, and Addresses. Edited by HIS CHILDREN. With Portrait and Illustrations. Crown 8vo, cloth, price 7s. 6d.

ALONE WITH THE WORD: Devotional Notes on the Whole of the New Testament. By G. STRINGER ROWE, Governor of Headingley College, Leeds. 8vo, cloth, price 6s. 6d.

WORKS BY CANON WYNNE, D.D.

I.

FRAGMENTARY RECORDS OF JESUS OF NAZARETH. From the Letters of a Contemporary. By FREDERICK R. WYNNE, D.D., Canon of Christ Church, and Incumbent of St. Matthias', Dublin. In crown 8vo, price 3s. 6d.

"Simple and yet forcible in style, the little volume is likely to lead the wavering to a firmer faith."—*Nonconformist.*
"This volume will be read with profit for its wisdom, excellent spirit, thorough fairness, and delightfully reverent tone."—*Christian Advocate.*

II.

THE JOY OF THE MINISTRY. An Endeavour to Increase the Efficiency and Deepen the Happiness of Pastoral Work. In crown 8vo, price 3s. 6d. Second Edition.

"There is no clergyman of any Church, old or young, who will not be moved, and there must be very few who will not be healthily stimulated, by the perusal of a work based on the purest Christian principles, and embodying in graceful language the results of wide observation and personal practice."—*Scotsman.*

III.

PLAIN PROOFS OF THE GREAT FACTS OF CHRISTIANITY. For the Help of Minds Perplexed with Difficulties. Cheap Edition. Cloth, price 1s. 6d.

IV.

SPENT IN THE SERVICE. A Memoir of the Very Rev. Achilles Daunt, D.D., Dean of Cork. With selections from his Letters, Diaries, and Sermons. Third Edition. With Portrait, price 5s.

"We feel grateful to Mr. Wynne for giving us so lifelike a sketch of a very beautiful character."—*Literary Churchman.*
"A most interesting memoir. Mr. Daunt appears to have been not only an eloquent and fervent preacher, but a most holy man, singularly true and thorough in all relations of life. The memoir is unusually well written, and readable."—*Guardian.*

CHRISTIAN THEISM: A Popular Survey of the Evidence on which it rests, and the Objections urged against it Considered and Refuted. By the Rev. Prebendary C. A. ROW, M.A., D.D. Crown 8vo, cloth, price 5s.

THE HALLOWING OF CRITICISM: Nine Cathedral Sermons on Elijah. By the Rev. Prof. T. K. CHEYNE, D.D., Canon of Rochester. Crown 8vo, cloth, price 5s.

PALESTINE IN THE TIME OF CHRIST. By EDMOND STAPFER, D.D., Professor in the Protestant Theological Faculty of Paris. Translated by ANNIE HARWOOD HOLMDEN. With Map. Crown 8vo, price 9s.

"The book, as a whole, is of great interest, and will prove, we believe, a great help to those who desire to reach for themselves the actual meaning of the Gospels. It will be a valuable addition to the *apparatus criticus* of the Biblical student, and will help to give colour and vividness to the preacher's description of scenes and incidents from which he would draw forth moral and spiritual lessons for his hearers."—*Nonconformist.*

THE TRINITY OF EVIL. I. INFIDELITY.—II. IMPURITY.—III. INTEMPERANCE. By Rev. Canon WILBERFORCE, M.A. New and Cheaper Edition. Crown 8vo, cloth, price 1s. 6d.

"One of the most sonorous and telling trumpet-blasts against infidelity, impurity, and intemperance we have ever heard. Every page of the Canon's not only throbs with passionate earnestness in the cause of truth and righteousness, but is full of point and fine literary power."—*Literary World.*

DANIEL'S PROPHECIES NOW BEING FULFILLED. With a Harmony in the Words of the Revised Version. By the Rev. E. P. CACHEMAILLE, M.A. In Crown 8vo, cloth, price 2s. 6d.

LIGHT AND COLOUR EMBLEMATIC OF REVEALED TRUTH. By the late Major R. W. D. NICKLE. Edited by SARAH SHARP. With Diagrams. Crown 8vo, cloth, price 7s. 6d.

"The work is highly edifying, and will be found by lovers of Holy Scripture to contain much that is fresh and instructive. The diagrams are choice, and tend greatly to the elucidation of the subject. By the help of this work a new domain of knowledge is opened, and many passages of Holy Writ re-illumined."—*Christian.*

SOME CENTRAL POINTS OF OUR LORD'S
MINISTRY. By the Rev. HENRY WACE, D.D., Principal of King's Coll., London, and Hon. Chaplain-in-Ordinary to the Queen; Author of "The Foundation of Faith," "Christianity and Morality," etc. Crown 8vo, cloth.

WORKS BY THE REV. CANON BELL, D.D., Rector of Cheltenham

OUR DAILY LIFE: Its Duties and its Dangers.
Crown 8vo, cloth, price 3s. 6d.

"The subjects selected are admirably handled. It is a very excellent, most useful book."—*Church Bells.*

HENRY MARTYN. Cheap Edition. Crown 8vo,
cloth, price 1s.

"A worthy record of a noble life."—*Whitehall Review.*
"In every way a most delightful volume."—*Rock.*

THE VALLEY OF WEEPING A PLACE
OF SPRINGS." A Practical Exposition of the Thirty-second Psalm. Crown 8vo, cloth, price 3s. 6d.

"The whole volume is delightful in every way. As a meditative work, it is one which will be profoundly enjoyed by those who can obtain a copy of it."—*Clergyman's Magazine.*

A WINTER ON THE NILE, IN EGYPT,
AND IN NUBIA. Second Edition. Artistically bound, Eau de Nil cloth, price 6s. With Map.

"He is an excellent traveller, making friends with everybody, receiving invitations from Egyptian authorities, foreign consuls, and Coptic clergy, and the native peasantry, all alike opening their hearts and homes to him. The result is an insight into Egypt as it is, and very much as it has been for a thousand years. The Canon's descriptions of manners and customs are lifelike, and sometimes not a little amusing."—*Times.*

GLEANINGS FROM A TOUR IN PALES-
TINE AND IN THE EAST. Second Edition. Crown 8vo, price 6s. With Map and Illustrations.

"Canon Bell is a scholar and something of a poet; and the reader may be sure that anything which proceeds from his hand is written with care, reverence, and polished skill. . . . It is a pleasant duty to recognise the admirable spirit in which Canon Bell has treated the more important part of his work. The reflections upon a visit to such spots as the Mount of Olives, the Garden of Gethsemane, or the place of the Crucifixion, are conceived in a truly reverent and majestic vein. The verses written in contemplation of these sacred spots are marked by great beauty and devotion. They read like some of the Church's glorious hymns of the Passion set anew, in fresh strains and varied metre."—*Morning Post.*

CHRIST AND HIS PEOPLE.
In crown 8vo, cloth, price 5s. Thirteen Addresses by

THE BISHOP OF LIVERPOOL, THE DEAN OF RIPON, ARCHDEACON RICHARDSON, CANON HOARE, PREBENDARY EDMONDS, H. C. G. MOULE, CANON J. W. BARDSLEY, SIR EMILIUS LAURIE, and GEORGE EVERARD.

THE REVELATION OF JOHN: An Exposition.
By P. W. GRANT, Author of "The Bible Record of Creation True for Every Age," "The Great Memorial Name," etc. Crown 8vo, cloth, price 6s.

THE SAINT AND HIS SAVIOUR.
By C. H. SPURGEON. A New Edition, set up and printed from new type. With Portrait. Crown 8vo, cloth, price 3s. 6d.

THE WOMEN FRIENDS OF JESUS;
or, Lives and Characters of the Holy Women of Gospel History. By HENRY C. McCOOK, D.D. In crown 8vo, cloth, price 5s.

"Dr. McCook describes in felicitous and flowery language the lives and characters of famous women of Gospel history."—*Scotsman*.

"Rich in Biblical and historical knowledge, and graphic and picturesque in style."—*Glasgow Herald*.

"It will be no difficult task to write many a paragraph in praise of the exquisite pathos, the insight into womanly character, which these pages breathe."—*Methodist Recorder*.

THE STORY OF THE LIFE OF JESUS
Told in Words Easy to Read and Understand. By the Author of "The Story of the Bible," etc. With Forty Illustrations. Handsomely bound, fcap. 4to, cloth, price 2s.

"An excellent Sunday book for children; the story is tenderly and brightly told, the pictures of Eastern life and Jewish manners form an effective running commentary on the text, which is interspersed besides with graphic views of the sacred cities, sites, and scenery."—*Times*.

TOILERS IN LONDON;
or, Enquiries Concerning Female Labour in the Metropolis. By the "BRITISH WEEKLY" COMMISSIONER. Crown 8vo, cloth, price 3s. 6d.

NEWLY ENLISTED.
A Series of Talks with Young Converts. By the Rev. THEODORE CUYLER, D.D. Square 16mo, 160 pp., cloth, price 1s. 6d.

"Clear, bright, forcible, these talks are full of wisdom. The book must rouse as well as teach many."—*Methodist Recorder*.

"This is a beautiful little volume, replete with sound thought, practical instruction, and earnest evangelical truth."—*Christian News*.

THE GROWTH OF CHURCH INSTITU-
TIONS. By Rev. EDWIN HATCH, D.D., Reader in Ecclesiastical History, Oxford. Second Edition. In crown 8vo, price 5s.

"Dr. Hatch's vast learning, his comprehensive grasp of his subject down to its minutest details, his lucid style, and his remarkable candour, are equally conspicuous, and we strongly commend the study and the mastery of this volume to all who are anxious to set the ecclesiastical problems of our day in their true light, and to resist the persistent claims of an arrogant priesthood."—*Freeman.*

THE ANGLICAN PULPIT OF TO-DAY.
Forty Short Biographies and Forty Sermons of Distinguished Preachers of the Church of England. In crown 8vo, price 7s. 6d. Handsomely bound in cloth.

DR. GODET'S BIBLICAL STUDIES.

I.

STUDIES ON THE NEW TESTAMENT.
By F. GODET, D.D., Professor of Theology, Neuchâtel. Edited by the Hon. and Rev. W. H. LYTTELTON, M.A., Canon of Gloucester. Seventh Edition. Crown 8vo, price 7s. 6d.

II.

STUDIES ON THE OLD TESTAMENT.
Fourth Edition. Crown 8vo, price 7s. 6d.

"Unquestionably M. Godet is one of the first, if not the very first, of contemporary commentators. We have no hesitation in advising all students of the Scripture to procure and to read with careful attention these luminous essays."—*Literary Churchman.*

WORKS BY PRINCIPAL FAIRBAIRN, D.D.

STUDIES IN THE LIFE OF CHRIST.
By A. M. FAIRBAIRN, D.D., Mansfield College, Oxford. Fifth Edition. 8vo, price 9s.

"These studies are full of spiritual penetration, profound philosophy of moral life, and literary beauty. Devout in feeling, and evangelical in theological view, they are yet characterised by great freedom and independence of thought."—*British Quarterly Review.*

THE CITY OF GOD.
A Series of Discussions in Religion. Third Edition. Price 7s. 6d.

"We have read many of the truly brilliant passages of this volume with thrilling delight. The theology is orthodox, the logic is accurate, and the learning profound."—*Ecclesiastical Gazette.*

RELIGION IN HISTORY AND IN THE
LIFE OF TO-DAY. Fourth Thousand. Cloth, price 1s. 6d.

"His clear and closely-reasoned thought finds utterance in clear and well-knit speech."—*Academy.*

THE MIRACLES OF OUR LORD. By the Rev.
Professor J. LAIDLAW, D.D., Author of "The Bible Doctrine of Man," etc. Crown 8vo, cloth, price 7s. 6d.

ROMANCE OF PSALTER AND HYMNAL:
Authors and Composers. By the Rev. R. E. WELSH, M.A., and F. G. EDWARDS, Author of "United Praise." Crown 8vo, cloth, price 6s.

TROPICAL AFRICA. By HENRY DRUMMOND,
F.R.S.E., F.G.S. Fifteenth Thousand. With Six Maps and Illustrations, price 6s.

"Professor Drummond is a clear and accurate observer, and as he has had a sound scientific training, and has a real interest in the human side of African life, he is able to present us with pictures of a distinctness and originality not often met with in books of African travel."—*Times.*

NATURAL LAW IN THE SPIRITUAL
WORLD. By Prof. HENRY DRUMMOND, F.R.S.E., F.G.S. Twenty-fifth Edition, completing Ninety-second Thousand. In crown 8vo, price 3s. 6d.

"This is one of the most impressive and suggestive books on religion that we have read for a long time. Indeed, with the exception of Dr. Mozeley's 'University Sermons,' we can recall no book of our time which showed such a power of re-stating the moral and practical truths of religion so as to make them take fresh hold of the mind and vividly impress the imagination."—*Spectator.*

THE GREATEST THING IN THE WORLD.
An Address on 1 Corinthians xiii. Crown 8vo, leatherette, price 1s.; cloth, 2s. 6d.

LECTURES ON THE HISTORY OF PREACH-
ING. By the late Rev. JOHN KER, D.D. Second Edition. Crown 8vo, price 7s. 6d.

"A valuable legacy to the Church of Christ. We know no better book than this to place in the hands of candidates for the ministry, and we should gladly see it used by the bishops of our own Church as an indispensable text-book for all who are studying for holy orders."—*English Churchman.*

JAMES MACDONELL OF "THE TIMES":
A Story of Self-Help. By W. ROBERTSON NICOLL, M.A. With Etched Portrait by H. Manesse. 8vo, price 12s.

MODERN SCIENCE IN BIBLE LANDS.
By Sir J. WILLIAM DAWSON, F.R.S. With Maps and Illustrations. In crown 8vo, price 9s.

"The result of a tour through Italy, Egypt, and Syria, collected by a geological observer of such eminence as Sir William Dawson has shown himself to be, cannot but be of great value. Such are his knowledge and grasp of the subject, his perfect fairness and impartiality, and his close and careful reasoning, that it is not too much to say that he has summed the present extent of our knowledge of Bible lands."—*Pall Mall Gazette.*

BY THE SAME AUTHOR.

I.

THE STORY OF THE EARTH AND MAN
With Twenty Illustrations. Ninth Edition. Crown 8vo, cloth, price 7s. 6d.

II.

FOSSIL MEN AND THEIR MODERN REPRE-
SENTATIVES. An attempt to illustrate the Characters and Condition of Pre-Historic Men in Europe by those of the American Races. With Forty-four Illustrations. Third Thousand. Crown 8vo, cloth, price 7s. 6d.

III.

THE ORIGIN OF THE WORLD, according to
Revelation and Science. Fifth Edition. Crown 8vo, cloth, price 7s. 6d.

"We heartily commend the book to all those who are interested in this most important question. Dr. Dawson is a man well known in the ranks of science for great breadth and grasp of knowledge; he has been a pioneer in geological discovery: he is also a considerable Hebrew scholar, well read in the Bible, and especially those parts which treat of nature. . . . It is a valuable addition to Bible criticism from a point of view higher scientifically than we have yet had."—*Spectator.*

WORKS BY DR. R. W. DALE, *Birmingham.*

IMPRESSIONS OF AUSTRALIA. Crown 8vo, cloth, price 5s.

LAWS OF CHRIST FOR COMMON LIFE.
Fourth Thousand. Crown 8vo, price 6s.

"Sound sense and wholesome Christian teaching conveyed in pure, idiomatic, and forcible English."—*Scotsman.*

"This book excellently well bears out its title. The author gives wise and manly counsel."—*Literary Churchman.*

THE EPISTLE TO THE EPHESIANS. Its
Doctrines and Ethics. Fourth Thousand. Crown 8vo, price 7s. 6d.

"In his first sermon as Vicar of Leeds, Dr. Talbot said: 'I believe that the thought of speaking of God's purpose in Christ was suggested to me by reading whilst abroad just now the impressive words about it in Dr. Dale's noble book upon the Epistle to the Ephesians. It is only a single but superlative instance of what we owe to Nonconformist faith and goodness.'"

THE NEW EVANGELICALISM AND THE
OLD. Crown 8vo, cloth, price 1s.

THE JEWISH TEMPLE AND THE
CHRISTIAN CHURCH. A Series of Discourses on the Epistle to the Hebrews. Seventh Edition. Crown 8vo, price 6s.

"Wholesomer sermons than these it is almost impossible to conceive. Mr. Dale's preaching has always been remarkable for moral energy and fervour, but here this characteristic rises to its highest power."—*Expositor.*

WEEK-DAY SERMONS. Fifth Edition. Crown 8vo, price 3s. 6d.

"Dr. Dale is certainly an admirable teacher of Christian ethics. He is, perhaps, the greatest living successor of the Apostle James. In this volume he appears at his best."—*Christian.*

THE TEN COMMANDMENTS. Fifth Edition.
Crown 8vo, price 5s.

"Full of thought and vigour."—*Spectator.*

"The manly, fearless honesty of Mr. Dale's Expositions demands the very highest eulogy."—*British Quarterly Review.*

NINE LECTURES ON PREACHING. Fifth
Edition. Crown 8vo, price 6s.

"Admirable lectures, briefly written, earnest and practical, the work of an able man."—*Literary Churchman.*

THE EVANGELICAL REVIVAL and other
Sermons. Crown 8vo, cloth, price 6s.

PROFESSOR KURTZ'S CHURCH HISTORY.

Authorised Translation from the latest revised edition, by the Rev. JOHN MACPHERSON, M.A. In three volumes. Price 7s. 6d. each

"The complete work of Professor Kurtz is now translated, and it really shows itself so improved in form, so much fuller in substance, in fact, so much changed in mind, body, and state, that it may claim to be a new history altogether. No one who has tried to peruse the original compilation will deny that this is an unspeakable advantage in a once unreadable manual; and, indeed, a 'manual,' by its very name, signifies a work that is meant to hold in the hand and not to enter the head. The author has carried on his history into the most recent days. Nothing has escaped his all-seeing eye and his all-recording pen—neither the Theosophism of Madame Blavatsky, nor the microscopic heresies of Mr. David Macrae in the United Presbyterian Church, neither the doings of the Berlin treaty nor of Dr. Robertson Smith. The annals of the last fifty years on the Continent are given with considerable fulness, and ecclesiastical events in Germany are given with an especial amount of detail."—*Scotsman.*

DR. FISHER'S NEW CHURCH HISTORY.

A HISTORY OF THE CHRISTIAN CHURCH.

By GEORGE P. FISHER, D.D., LL.D., Professor of Ecclesiastical History in Yale University. In large 8vo, 712 pages, price 12s. With Seven coloured Maps.

"This very valuable and exhaustive history."—*English Churchman.*

"It is a book as remarkable for fairness and breadth of sympathy as it is for learning and power; and if its popularity should be as great as its value, is success is assured."—*Nonconformist.*

THE CATACOMBS OF ROME, AND THEIR TESTIMONY RELATIVE TO PRIMITIVE CHRISTIANITY. By Rev. W. H. WITHROW, M.A. Crown 8vo, cloth, price 6s. 560 pages, 134 Illustrations.

"An exceedingly painstaking and thorough-going work, and whether or not the writer may be correct in all his inferences, they have evidently been founded upon diligent information. He could not have very much that was absolutely new to tell on the subject; but as a convenient account of the most remarkable and interesting monuments of primitive Christianity, of those excavations which furnished the persecuted Church with refuges during life and in death, which formed her places of worship in times of peril, and received the remains of martyrs, the present volume is perhaps inferior to none of its predecessors."—*Saturday Review.*

THE PHILANTHROPY OF GOD. By the Rev. HUGH PRICE HUGHES, M.A. Crown 8vo, cloth, price 3s. 6d.

SOCIAL CHRISTIANITY. Sermons delivered in St. James's Hall, London. By Rev. HUGH PRICE HUGHES, M.A. Third Edition. In crown 8vo, cloth, price 3s. 6d.

PRESS NOTICES.

"If all sermons were as fresh and unconventional, as simple, practical, and unaffected as those which he (Rev. Hugh Price Hughes) has put together under the appropriate title of 'Social Christianity,' there would perhaps be less grumbling from the pew than is at present the case."—*Scotsman.*

"Wise, strong, wholesome, and thoughtful."—*British Weekly.*

"It is not difficult, after reading these fervid, brave, and genial addresses, to understand the secret of such a preacher's spell. Mr. Price Hughes does not mince matters in dealing with the lawlessness, the Mammon-Worship, and the social disorders of the times; and the tones in which he speaks are far-reaching and persuasive, because they are brotherly and full of faith and hope."—*Leeds Mercury.*

"These vigorous sermons are an attempt to show that what must be called the social failure of Christianity is not the fault of Christianity or of Christ, but rather the result of Christians having been selfishly individualistic. The great evils of our day, and especially those of our own country, are brought to view with much directness, and the duties and responsibilities of disciples of Christ are enforced with plainness and power. Whether the subject be social distress, the administration of justice, Christ's authority, or the problem of unbelief, we find these pages uniformly practical and in a high degree instructive."—*Christian.*

"These sermons are full of good, manly, vigorous teaching of a stout, practical kind."—*Star.*

"While the ordinary volume of sermons sends people to sleep, this will assuredly keep them awake; and it will, moreover, keep them awake by perfectly legitimate expedients."—*Manchester Examiner.*

THE ATHEIST SHOEMAKER: A Story of the West End Mission. By the Rev. HUGH PRICE HUGHES, M.A. Crown 8vo, cloth, price 1s. 6d.

JOHN G. PATON: An Autobiography. Second Part. Edited by his Brother, the Rev. JAMES PATON, B.A. Sixth Thousand. Crown 8vo, cloth, price 6s.

JOHN G. PATON, Missionary to the New Hebrides. An Autobiography. Edited by HIS BROTHER. With Portrait. Fifth Edition, completing Eleventh Thousand. Crown 8vo, cloth, price 6s.

The Rev. Dr. PIERSON, author of "The Crisis of Missions," savs : "I consider it *unsurpassed* in missionary biography. In the whole course of my extensive reading on these topics, a more stimulating, inspiring, and every way first-class book has not fallen into my hands. Everybody ought to read it."

OPINIONS OF THE PRESS.

"A more fascinating and thrilling bit of Missionary history has seldom been given to the public."—*Christian.*

"Intensely interesting; indeed, often quite fascinating."—*Christian Leader.*

"Let the people who tell us that the romance of missions is passed, read this manly and thrilling narrative. . . No fiction can exercise a stronger spell than the story of this brave Cameronian missionary's life."—*Baptist Magazine.*

"The story of Mr. Paton's years of residence among the Tannese, amid many perils and great discouragements, is quite as fascinating in some parts as many a romance. The author, indeed, seems to have passed through dangers and difficulties which it would be hard to believe were the veracity of the writer not beyond question. . . . An autobiography recording the life and work of a missionary in some respects not unlike his great prototype—David Livingstone."—*Scotsman.*

"He has a story to tell that is well worth hearing, and that at not a few stages will compare handsomely with most books of adventure."—*Scottish Leader.*

"We recommend it to all our missionary societies as a most convincing testimony to the value of Gospel work among the heathen."—*Methodist Times.*

"Simplicity and godly sincerity are stamped on every page."—*Leeds Mercury.*

"This is a book far beyond our praise. It will take its place with the classics of missions—with the Lives of Brainerd and Martyn, and the other records which will endure as long as Christ is preached. Great as has been the missionary work accomplished by the author, we believe it will be found in the end that his greatest work has been the writing of this volume. It is a book which cannot be read without indescribable emotion. . . . It must surely, now and in days to come, kindle in many souls something of the writer's own lofty and fervent love. More than any argument it will silence the faithless clamour against missions; and no one, Christian or sceptic, will peruse it without feeling that there is amongst us still at least one truly Apostolic man." *British Weekly.*

CHARLES STANFORD, D.D.: Memories and Letters. Edited by HIS WIFE. With Etched Portrait by MANESSE. Crown 8vo, cloth, price 5s.

THE PREACHER'S COMMENTARY ON THE GOSPEL OF ST. JOHN. A Series of One Hundred and Thirty Homiletic Sketches. By the Rev. GEORGE CALTHROP, M.A., Vicar of St. Augustine, Highbury. In crown 8vo, cloth, price 3s. 6d.

"His general method of describing and drawing lessons from the events of our Lord's life is vivid and interesting."—*Guardian.*

"A very suitable handbook for suggestions in a course of sermons or lectures on the fourth Gospel."—*Ecclesiastical Gazette.*

THE BRITISH WEEKLY PULPIT. Vol. I. 624 pages, 8vo, handsomely bound in cloth, red edges, price 6s.

Contains only first-rate matter, having regard not to quantity, but quality, and includes Sermons, etc., from the Provinces, Wales and Scotland, as well as from Ireland; and numerous articles of varied interest and importance, and sermons by the following and many other preachers:—

Revs. J. B. Meharry, C. H. Spurgeon, G. Matheson, D.D., Principal Fairbairn, D.D., A. Martin, M.A., Professor Godet, D.D., Dr. Oswald Dykes, A. Mursell, Prof. R. Flint, D.D., Dr. Dallinger, T. Champness, A. Whyte, D.D.. Prof. Knight, LL.D., Joseph Parker, D.D., A. Maclaren, D.D., Principal T. C. Edwards, D.D., Jno. Pulsford, D.D., Bishop Alexander, D.D., John McNeill, Adolph Saphir, D.D., W. C. Smith, D.D., John Watson, M.A., Dr. MacGregor, Prof. Elmslie, D.D., J. Culross, D.D., W. B. Robertson, D.D., R. W. Dale, LL.D., C. A. Berry.

THE INDUSTRIES OF JAPAN. Together with an account of its Agriculture, Forestry, Mining, Arts, and Commerce. By Prof. J. J. REIN, University of Bonn. Illustrated by Woodcuts, Lithographs, and Native Fabrics. In one Handsome Volume. Royal 8vo, price 30s. With Forty-four Illustrations and Three Maps.

"Professor Rein is equally exhaustive whatever subject or branch of a subject may be under review, and his book is a perfect mine of information of a most valuable and interesting kind."—*Scotsman.*

JAPAN. Travels and Researches undertaken at the cost of the Prussian Government. With Twenty Illustrations and Two Maps. By the SAME AUTHOR. Second Edition. Uniform in Size and Type. Price 25s.

"No existing work on Japan can pretend to vie with the present one in the fulness and accuracy with which the physiography, natural history, and topography of the country—subjects which Dr. Rein has made specially his own—are treated; and for a long time to come it must rank as the standard authority in such matters."—*Spectator.*

"It is the most important and exhaustive work that has yet appeared on the physiography of that interesting land. The work of translation is excellently done under the supervision of the author."—*Westminster Review.*

WORKS BY THE REV. PROF. A. B. BRUCE, D.D.

I.
THE MIRACULOUS ELEMENT IN THE GOSPELS. In 8vo, cloth, price 12s.

"It displays minute acquaintance with the modern literature of the subject, and all forms of attack to which Christian belief in the supernatural has been subjected. The defence is able all round; and the closing chapters—in which the miracle implied in the character of Jesus is dwelt on, and where the defence is for a moment changed into attack—are full of spirit and fire."—*Methodist Recorder.*

II.
THE CHIEF END OF REVELATION.
Third Thousand. In crown 8vo, cloth, price 6s.

"Dr. Bruce has given us a contribution of very great value. Like everything else that has come from his pen, this series of lectures has the conspicuous excellence of boldness, vigour, breadth, and moral elevation."—*Professor Salmond.*

III.
THE PARABOLIC TEACHING OF CHRIST:
A Systematic and Critical Study of the Parables of our Lord. Second Edition. 8vo, cloth, price 12s.

"Professor Bruce brings to his task the learning and the liberal and finely sympathetic spirit which are the best gifts of an expositor of Scripture. His treatment of his subject is vigorous and original."—*Spectator.*

IV.
THE LIFE OF WILLIAM DENNY, Shipbuilder,
Dumbarton. With Portrait. Second Edition. 8vo, cloth, price 12s.

"A most interesting biography."—*Academy.*

"Dr. Bruce could not have found a worthier subject for his first essay in biography, and William Denny could not have had a more congenial biographer."—*British Weekly.*

"Professor Bruce has shown remarkable skill . . . this admirable 'Life.'"—*Scotsman*

CHRISTIAN CONDUCT Sermons delivered in the
Chapel of Mill Hill School by the Headmaster, C. A. VINCE, M.A. Crown 8vo, cloth, price 5s.

PRECIOUS SEED SOWN IN MANY
LANDS. Sermons by the Rev. A. N. SOMERVILLE, D.D. With a Biographical Sketch and Portrait. Crown 8vo, cloth, price 5s.

IRELAND AND THE CELTIC CHURCH.
A History of Ireland from St. Patrick to the English Conquest in 1172. By Rev. G. T. STOKES, M.A., Professor of Ecclesiastical History in the University of Dublin, and Rector of All Saints, Blackrock. Second Edition. Crown 8vo, cloth, price 9s.

"Any one who can make the dry bones of ancient Irish history live again may feel sure of finding an audience, sympathetic, intelligent, and ever-growing. Dr. Stokes has this faculty in a high degree. This book will be a boon to that large and growing number of persons who desire to have a trustworthy account of the beginning of Irish history, and cannot study it for themselves in the great but often dull works of the original investigators. It collects the scattered and often apparently insignificant results of original workers in this field, interprets them for us, and brings them into relation with the broader and better known facts of European history."—*Westminster Review.*

FORESHADOWINGS OF CHRISTIANITY.
By JOSEPHINE PECKOVER. With Preface by ANNE W. RICHARDSON, B.A. In crown 8vo, cloth, price 5s.

RAYS OF MESSIAH'S GLORY; or, Christ in
the Old Testament. By DAVID BARON. Second Edition. Crown 8vo, cloth, price 3s. 6d.

HUMAN DESTINY. By ROBERT ANDERSON, LL.D.,
Barrister-at-Law, Assistant Commissioner of Police of the Metropolis. Second and Cheaper Edition. Price 3s. 6d.

"It is seldom that we take up a book of which we wish that it had been longer, but Dr. Anderson's is such a book. It summarises the conflict through which the writer passed in studying the question of the destiny of the lost. It is refreshing to read a work which goes fairly to the very root of each theory in turn, and so states the issues involved in it that the reader can easily form his own conclusions. His book contains much that is valuable, and is loyal throughout to the teachings of Scripture."—*Record.*

THE COMING PRINCE: The Last Great Monarch
of Christendom. By the SAME AUTHOR. Third Edition. Crown 8vo, price 5s.

"The clearest exposition of the Seventy Weeks of Daniel that we have ever read."—*Gospel Watchman.*
"Deeply interesting from the first page to the last."—*Home Words.*

WORKS BY REV. MARCUS DODS, D.D.

I.
MOHAMMED, BUDDHA, AND CHRIST.
Fifth Thousand. Crown 8vo, cloth, price 3s. 6d.

"His materials have been carefully collected from the best sources, have been thoroughly digested in his own mind, and are here given forth to his readers in well-arranged, clear, and precise language."—*Scotsman.*

"Its general truth few reflecting Christians will doubt, and its elevating tendency nobody, Christian or unbeliever, will deny. To us this book is specially welcome, as an evidence, in addition to many others, of a new outburst of earnest religious thought and sentiment."—*Spectator.*

II.
ISRAEL'S IRON AGE: Sketches from the Period
of the Judges. Fourth Edition. Crown 8vo, cloth, price 5s.

"Powerful lectures. This is a noble volume, full of strength. Young men especially will find in it a rich storehouse of prevailing incentive to a godly life. Dr. Dods searches with a masterly hand."—*Nonconformist.*

III.
THE PRAYER THAT TEACHES TO PRAY.
Sixth Edition. Crown 8vo, price 2s. 6d.

"A warm welcome will be given by many to this little book. It is a book to be read in the closet, and from the perusal of which no one can rise without a quickened spiritual life. Unquestionably it will add to the author's reputation."—*Literary World.*

"It is highly instructive, singularly lucid, and unmistakably for quiet personal use."—*Clergyman's Magazine.*

WORKS BY REV. DR. W. M. TAYLOR, New York.

THE PARABLES OF OUR SAVIOUR EXPOUNDED AND ILLUSTRATED. In crown 8vo, cloth, price 7s. 6d.

"We have many books on the parables of our Lord, but few which so thoroughly as this condense within their covers the best teaching contained in the various commentaries written to elucidate their meaning. Dr. Taylor is not, however, a slavish imitator of any master in Israel; he has thought out his subject for himself, and gives us a real exposition in eloquent language, such as will be valued by Bible students."—*English Churchman.*

THE LIMITATIONS OF LIFE, AND OTHER
SERMONS. Second Edition. Crown 8vo, cloth, price 7s. 6d.

"Dr. Taylor's sermons are full of spiritual earnestness and power."—*London Quarterly Review.*

CONTRARY WINDS, AND OTHER SERMONS. Crown 8vo, price 7s. 6d.

JOHN KNOX. Price 1s.

"A short biography, which has two great merits—it presents in short compass, and yet in their true proportions, all the important events of the Reformer's life; and the warm appreciation of Knox's character and achievements by which it is pervaded is never allowed to descend to the level of mere undiscriminating eulogy."—*Scotsman.*

VENI CREATOR: Thoughts on the Holy Spirit of Promise. By the Rev. H. C. G. MOULE, M.A., Principal of Ridley Hall, Cambridge, Author of "Outlines of Christian Doctrine," etc. Crown 8vo, cloth, price 5s.

THE VOICES OF THE PSALMS. By the Right Rev. W. PAKENHAM WALSH, D.D., Lord Bishop of Ossory, Author of "The Moabite Stone," etc. Crown 8vo, cloth, price 5s.

CONTENTS — INTRODUCTORY — VOICES OF PRAISE — VOICES OF PRAYER—VOICES OF INSTRUCTION—VOICES OF CREATION—VOICES OF HISTORY—VOICES OF IMMORTALITY—VOICES OF THE SANCTUARY—VOICES OF MUSIC—VOICES OF THE SHEPHERD, THE WARRIOR, AND THE OUTLAW—VOICES OF THE MONARCH, THE PENITENT, AND THE PILGRIM—VOICES OF THE MESSIAH, THE KING, THE PROPHET AND PRIEST—VOICES OF REDEMPTION—VOICES OF THE CHURCH—VOICES OF THE MISSION FIELD—VOICES OF THE SPIRITUAL LIFE—VOICES OF BENEDICTION.

JOINTS IN OUR SOCIAL ARMOUR. By JAMES RUNCIMAN, Author of "A Dream of the North Sea," etc. Crown 8vo, cloth, price 5s.

CONTENTS—THE ETHICS OF THE DRINK QUESTION—VOYAGING AT SEA—WAR—DRINK—CONCERNING PEOPLE WHO KNOW THEY ARE GOING WRONG—THE SOCIAL INFLUENCE OF THE "BAR"—FRIENDSHIP—DISASTERS AT SEA—A RHAPSODY OF SUMMER—LOST DAYS—MIDSUMMER DAYS AND NIGHTS—DANDIES—GENIUS AND RESPECTABILITY—SLANG—PETS—THE ETHICS OF THE TURF, ETC.—DISCIPLINE—BAD COMPANY—GOOD COMPANY—GOING A-WALKING—"SPORT"—DEGRADED MEN—A REFINEMENT OF "SPORTING" CRUELTY.

MEMORIALS OF EDWIN HATCH, D.D.,
sometime Reader in Ecclesiastical History in the University of Oxford, and Rector of Purleigh. Edited by HIS BROTHER. With Portrait. Crown 8vo, cloth, 7s. 6d.

TOWARDS FIELDS OF LIGHT: Sacred Poems.
By the late Rev. EDWIN HATCH, D.D. Crown 8vo, cloth, gilt edges, 2s. 6d.

"The high level of merit sustained throughout will insure a deep interest among lovers of devotional verse. These poems maintain the traditions of the best English religious poetry."—*Scotsman.*

"They are exquisitely beautiful."—*Church Review.*
"These delicate and thoughtful poems breathe the very spirit of their author, broad, simple, and sincere."—*Pall Mall Gazette.*

THE MAKERS OF MODERN ENGLISH.
By the Rev. W. J. DAWSON, Author of "The Threshold of Manhood," etc. Crown 8vo, cloth, price 5s.

CONTENTS—INTRODUCTORY—THE INTERVAL BEFORE THE DAWN—ROBERT BURNS—LORD BYRON—PERCY BYSSHE SHELLEY—JOHN KEATS—SIR WALTER SCOTT—COLERIDGE—ROBERT SOUTHEY—WILLIAM WORDSWORTH—WORDSWORTH'S LIFE AND POETRY—SOME CHARACTERISTICS OF HIS POETRY, ETC.—THE HUMANITARIAN MOVEMENT IN POETRY: THOMAS HOOD AND MRS. BROWNING—LORD TENNYSON: GENERAL CHARACTERISTICS—TREATMENT OF NATURE—LOVE AND WOMAN, ETC.—ROBERT BROWNING—BROWNING'S PHILOSOPHY OF LIFE—THE SPIRIT OF BROWNING'S RELIGION, ETC.—MATTHEW ARNOLD—D. G. ROSSETTI—A. C. SWINBURNE—WILLIAM MORRIS.

PROFESSOR W. G. ELMSLIE, D.D.: Memoir

and Remains. Edited by W. ROBERTSON NICOLL, M.A., LL.D., Editor of *The Expositor*. With Portrait, crown 8vo, cloth, price 6s.

RESCUERS AND RESCUED: Experiences among

our City Poor. By the Rev. JAMES WELLS, M.A., Glasgow, Author of "Christ and the Heroes of Christendom," etc. Crown 8vo, cloth, price 3s. 6d.

UNTIL THE DAY BREAK, and Other Hymns

and Poems. By the late Rev. HORATIUS BONAR, D.D. Crown 8vo, price 5s.

CONTENTS—GENERAL HYMNS—CHRISTMAS AND NEW YEARS' HYMNS—HYMNS OF ISRAEL—FRAGMENTS.

A VALUABLE TEXT BOOK.

OUTLINES OF CHRISTIAN DOCTRINE.

By the Rev. H. C. G. MOULE, M.A., Principal of Ridley Hall, Cambridge. Third Edition, with new Indexes. Fcap. 8vo. Price 2s. 6d.

The *Guardian* says: " Mr. Moule has attempted a very difficult task, and has at least succeeded in condensing an immense mass of information into a small compass. It is perhaps superfluous to say that his work is characterized by great reverence from the first page to the last. At every point the reader feels that he is reading a statement of theology which is the life of the writer. In the more strictly theological part the summary is, as a rule, arranged and expressed excellently."

Crown 8vo, cloth, price 7s. 6d.

LIFE INSIDE THE CHURCH OF ROME.

By M. F. CLARE CUSACK, "The Nun of Kenmare."

NOTICES OF THE PRESS.

"Miss Cusack has a great deal to reveal, and she speaks with no hesitating sound. The book before us is something more than a revalation to the Protestant world; it is also a controversial treatise, in popular form, in which the doctrinal errors of the Papacy are considered from the highest standpoint—the written Word of God. It is a book which should find a place on every Protestant family's bookshelves."—*English Churchman.*

"Deserves to receive the earnest consideration of all who have any care whatever for the welfare of their country. More than anything else its pages ought to open the eyes of the ritualists."—*City Press.*

"We are not aware that there has been published any work which has exposed the inner life and working of the Roman Church as does the present volume. It is surprising to see what a keen insight Miss Cusack has into the whole Romish system—political, social, and literary."—*Rock.*

"This most interesting, important, and even sensational book. . . . We heartily commend it, and thank most heartily the talented authoress for her faithfulness in revealing the hidden evils of Romanism."
Protestant Observer.

"Some of the instances related by Miss Cusack are heartrending. The Romish Church to-day, as ever, is built on lies, forgeries, shameless misrepresentations of history and the positions of opponents, and suppressions of the truth."—*Christian World.*

"If there be any belated Protestant in the present day who thinks that the Papal Apostasy is a branch of the true Church of Christ, and that it is capable of being used by God as an instrument for the elevation of mankind, we would advise him to read the Nun of Kenmare's new book. Miss Cusack, like many others, was beguiled for a season, but painful experience opened her eyes to the true nature of this cleverly devised, but corrupt and tyrannical organisation. It is clear from her recital that the continued existence of Popery as a religious (or rather, irreligious) system, rests on the dense ignorance of its votaries. Even a slight knowledge of revealed truth would be fatal to the pretensions of the Papacy. The author tells us that the best educated of Roman Catholics are entirely ignorant of the Bible. The great duty of the hour is to enlighten these unhappy people as to the true nature of the system that enslaves them. Under the circumstances, that is no easy task, but we are hopeful that it is being gradually accomplished; and Miss Cusack's book would go far to bring it about if the mass of Romanists could have the opportunity of reading it."—*Christian.*

www.ingramcontent.com/pod-product-compliance
Lightning Source LLC
Chambersburg PA
CBHW031352230426
43670CB00006B/519